An Art Appreciation Primer

Elements and Principles of Design

First Edition

By Jennifer Snyder
Austin Peay State University

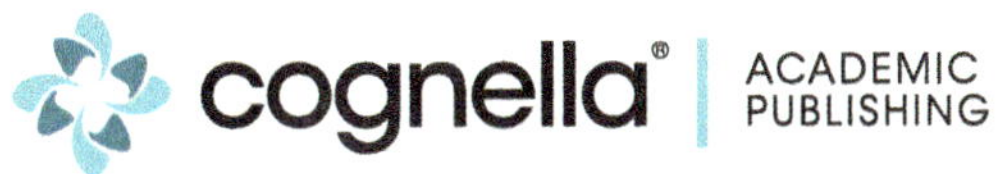

Bassim Hamadeh, CEO and Publisher
Kassie Graves, Director of Acquisitions
Jamie Giganti, Senior Managing Editor
Miguel Macias, Senior Graphic Designer
Zina Craft, Senior Field Acquisitions Editor
Gem Rabanera, Project Editor
Elizabeth Rowe, Licensing Coordinator
Chelsey Schmid, Associate Editor

Printed in the United States of America

ISBN: 978-1-5165-0580-7 (pbk) / 978-1-5165-0581-4 (br)

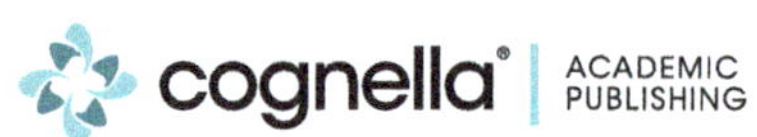

Table of Contents

Introduction

The Elements and Principles of Design

WHAT ARE THE ELEMENTS AND PRINCIPLES OF DESIGN?

There are as many explanations as to what the elements and principles of design are as there are textbooks, articles, and websites dedicated to one, some, or all of them. At the end of the day the elements and principles of design consist of a series of ideas and design principles meant to help the viewer and artist navigate through a composition in a way that makes explanations easier to understand.

One of the best descriptions of the elements and principles comes from j6design: "The elements and principles of design are the building blocks. The elements of design are the things that make up a design. The principles of design are what we do to those elements. How we apply the principles of design determines how successful the design is." (http://www.j6design.com.au/6-principles-of-design/)

The purpose of this workbook is to provide a succinct description of the elements and principles of design so that students have a clear understanding of their use in art appreciation and art history classes. My experience teaching art appreciation courses for the last ten years is that students learn the definitions of the elements and principles of design but often struggle with applying that knowledge to an actual work of art. The examples chosen for this text will show a clear connection between the definition and real-world examples from a variety of cultures and art forms.

The exercises included in this text are designed so that artists of all skill levels can practice applying the elements and principles in a way that makes sense for the beginning artist or art scholar. I find it is often through the practical hands-on experimentation with form that students come to a greater understanding of what it means to apply the elements and principles of design to a work of art.

The elements of design are generally considered to be:

- Line
- Shape and mass
- Light and color
- Space
- Time and Motion
- Texture

The principles of design are:

- Unity and variety
- Emphasis and subordination
- Balance
- Rhythm and repetition
- Contrast
- Scale and proportion

Chapter 1

The Visual Elements: Line

DEFINITION AND TYPES

Line is considered by many to be the most basic element of art. Line is the extension of a point. For many artists, line is the beginning of their drawing process. Line can come in many forms: horizontal, diagonal, vertical, zigzag, wavy, curved, broken, dashed, or implied.

Horizontal lines are seen within a composition as being calm and serene. Think of a landscape or the horizon, and you have a good example of a horizontal line within a composition. ***Vertical*** lines are often used to imply height or directional movement. They are more dynamic than horizontal lines but less dynamic than diagonal lines. ***Diagonal*** lines are seen as the most dynamic of the three basic forms of line and are often used to show action or movement within a composition (Figure 1.1).

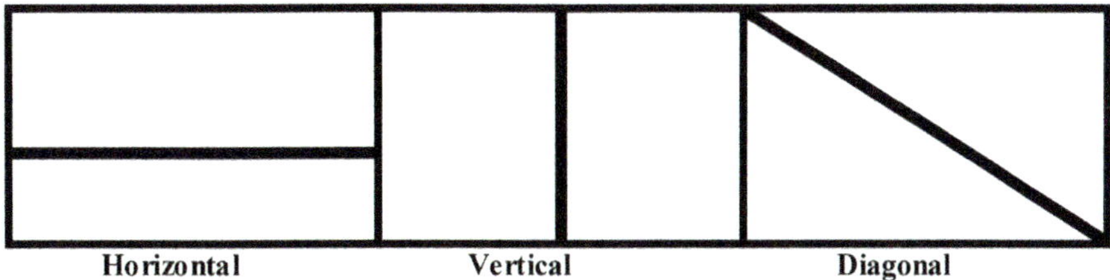

FIG. 1.1 Jennifer Snyder, *Line*. The three basic forms of line.

Lines can be used to indicate direction, define a form, create a shape, or indicate value and light within a two-dimensional work.

Boats at Saintes-Maries by Vincent van Gogh is an excellent example of the use of ***line*** as a means of showing movement (Figure 1.2). Throughout the composition van Gogh creates the effect of water in motion simply by varying the width and direction of the lines. While most of the lines in question are wavy, those lines that are implying whitecaps on the waves are more frenzied and contain small dashes, creating the effect of churning movement. The effect of distance is created through the use of smaller and smaller lines as the water approaches the horizon line. The sky is filled with small dashes of line in part to differentiate it from the wavy lines used in the water. The use of darker color in the lines of the boats help make them stand out against the lighter color of the water.

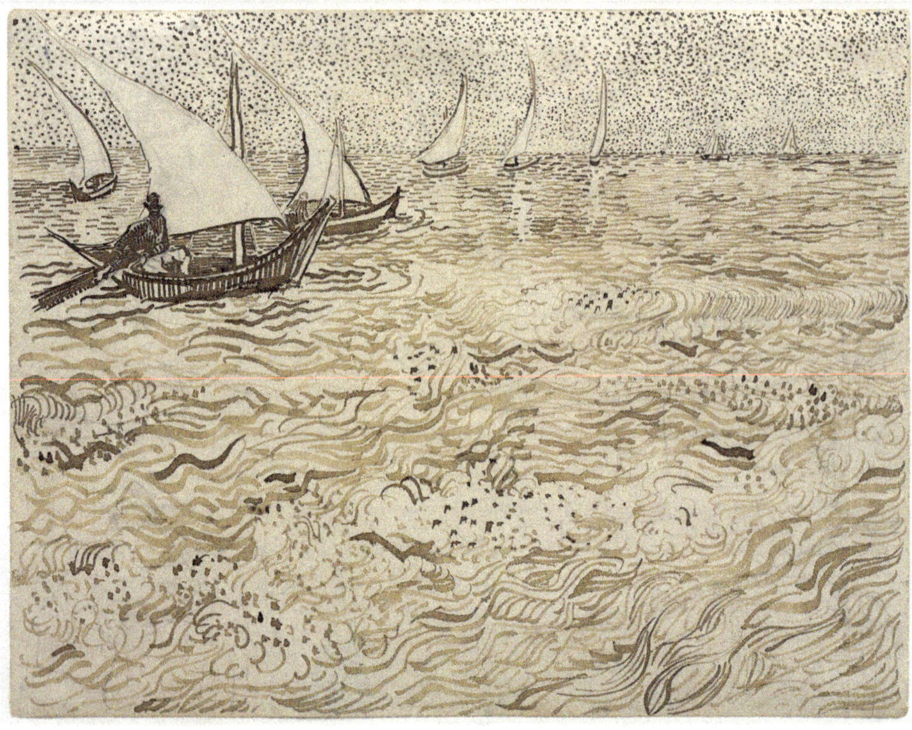

FIG. 1.2 Example of line. Vincent van Gogh, Boats at Saintes-Maries, 1888. Reed pen and ink over graphite on wove paper, 24.3 x 31.9 cm. Solomon R. Guggenheim Museum, New York. Thannhauser Collection, Gift, Justin K. Thannhauser, 1978. Copyright in the Public Domain.

Contour lines are lines that show where an object starts and stops. Contour lines are often referred to as outlines and are used to define shape. ***Hatching*** and ***cross-hatching*** are types of lines that are used to create texture, value, and the illusion of light and form within a composition. Hatching lines are parallel to one another while cross-hatching lines intersect one another. ***Stippling*** is a technique in which small dots or marks are used to define form. ***Implied lines*** are lines that are not actually present in the composition but are indicated by value, colors, textures, or shapes which lead the viewer through the artwork (Figure 1.3).

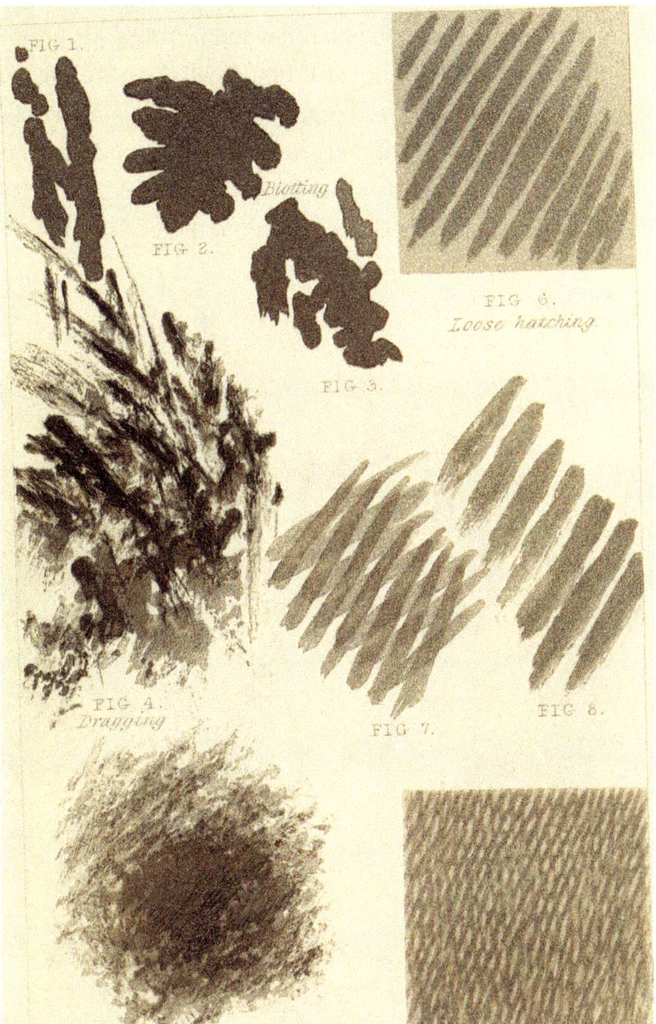

FIG. 1.3 Hatching and cross hatching. This sketchbook page shows a variety of drawing techniques using watercolor paint. Hatching and crosshatching are both detailed in this illustration. S.T. Whiteford. Copyright in the Public Domain.

Line quality refers to the type of mark making used by the artist in the composition. Line quality is sometimes referred to as line weight and is the thickness or thinness of the line. Thicker lines can be used to indicate where an object is heavier or darker within a composition. For example, lines in areas of shadow are often thicker than lines in areas of lightness. Line quality adds visual interest to an artwork by adding variety to the drawing of an object within a work of art.

Dancers by Ernst Ludvig Kirchner uses a variety of line widths and styles to create the effect of movement in the dancers onstage. The use of zigzag lines helps create the illusion of crinolines in the underskirts of the dancers, while the thicker black lines in their bloomers help them be seen as ruffled. The use of black on the stockings of the dancers, as well as the way the dancers are posed, with their right legs lifted up to show their underskirts creates a sense of motion and ***implied line*** (Figure 1.4). The eye of the viewer follows the dark line created by the stationary legs up to the pointed toe of the raised leg. Although this is not a true line, it is implied and reads as a continuous line in the composition. The use of thinner lines in the remainder of the image reinforces the idea that the legs of the dancers should be the focal point of the composition.

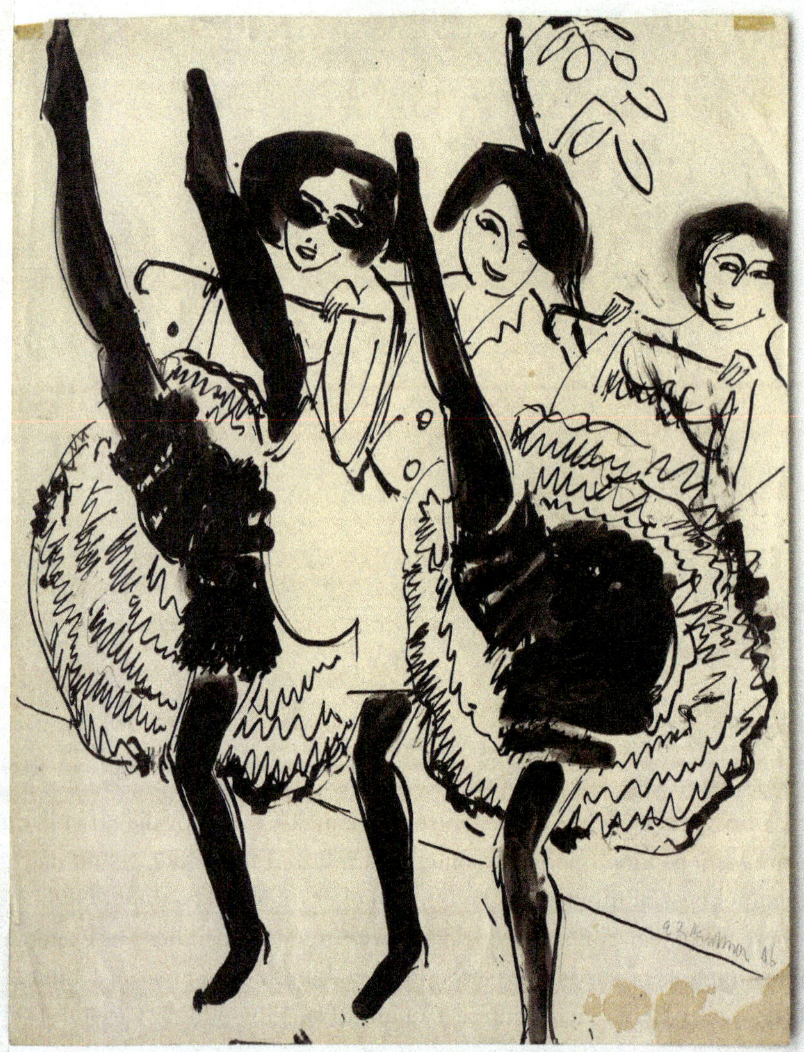

FIG. 1.4 Example of implied line. Ernst Ludwig Kirchner, Dancers, 1906. Ink on paper, 44.8 x 34.9 cm. Solomon R. Guggenheim Museum, New York. Copyright in the Public Domain.

PROJECT IDEAS

Types of Line

There are a variety of lines artists can use in their work. Some of these lines include: horizontal, diagonal, perpendicular, parallel, straight, curved, wavy, zigzag, dashed, or dotted. Create an abstract image using at least three of the types of line listed above.

Line Weight

Line weight is the relative heaviness, strength, or darkness of a line in an image. Different types of drawing implements create different line weights due to the thickness or darkness of the line they can make. A ballpoint pen, for example, would create a much lighter line weight than a marker of the same thickness. Create a grid using at least nine squares. Using at least three different types of drawing implements, demonstrate three different types of line weight for each implement.

Creating Pattern

Pattern is a repetition of elements within a design. A checkerboard is an example of a simple pattern using color variation. Combining types of line and line weight, create at least four simple patterns. Color may be added after the pattern is completed, but the focus of the drawing should be on the creation of the patterns.

Chapter 2

Shape and Mass

DEFINITION AND TYPES

Two-dimensional v. three-dimensional

Two-dimensional (2D) shape is the outer edges or outline of an object on a flat surface. The outline of an apple drawn on paper would be considered two-dimensional. In actuality, anything on a flat surface is two-dimensional in that the projection of the object into "space" is merely an illusion of perspective (Figure 2.1, page 10).

This work by Kazimir Malevich, *Suprematist Composition,* uses ***shape*** and implied mass, but actual mass is absent. The simple shapes used in this composition, squares and rectangles, are the type of geometric works for which Malevich is known. The overlapping of the shapes, such as the blue square overlapping the black rectangle, creates a sense of space in the composition where there is none. The space (volume) is implied and not actual.

Three-dimensional (3D) shape, on the other hand, is the creation of an actual object that exists in space. Any work of art not on paper or canvas could

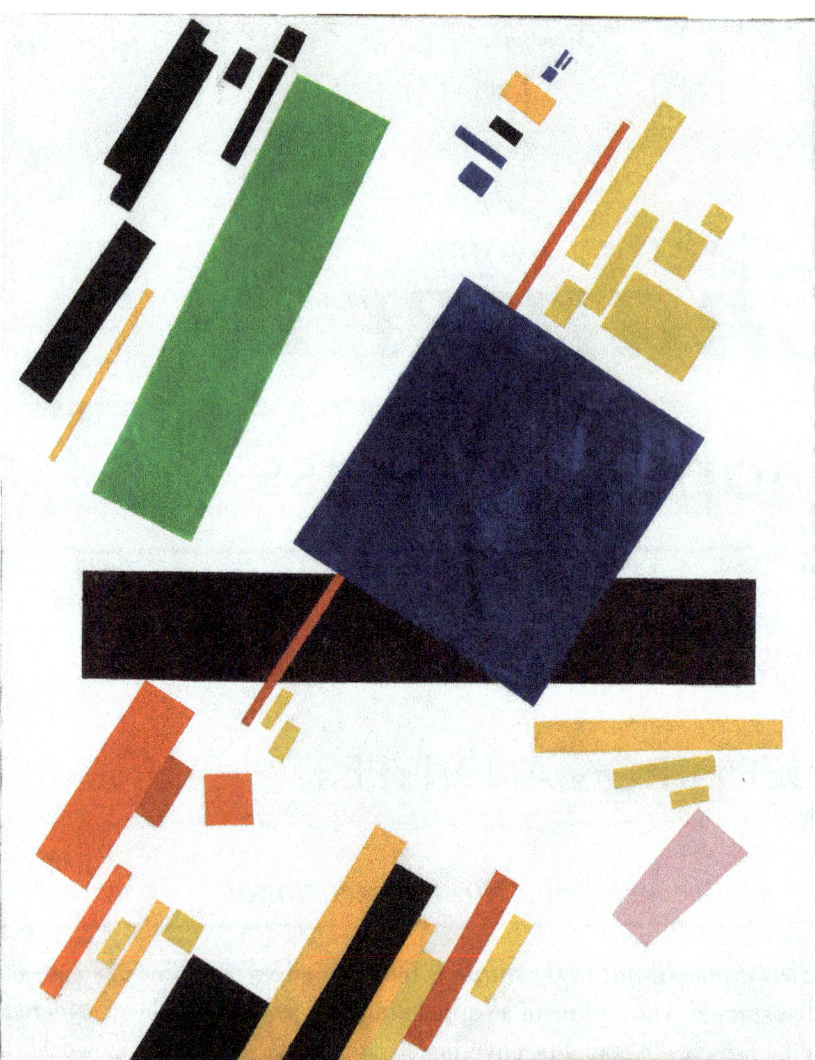

FIG. 2.1 Example of shape. Kazimir Malevich, Suprematist composition (blue rectangle over purple beam), 1916. Oil on canvas. 88 × 70.5 cm. Copyright in the Public Domain.

be considered three-dimensional, but certainly sculpture, ceramics, and any other utilitarian objects would qualify as three-dimensional. Three-dimensional forms have mass.

Open Form v. Closed Form

In sculpture, ***open form*** is a type of sculpture that includes either naturally occurring spaces in the artwork or the extension of part of the sculpture into space away from the main part of the sculpture. A sculpture of a person with one arm extended in space would be considered open form, as would a sculpture with the naturally occurring open spaces in the body, such as the space between the legs. These spaces would not be filled with the surrounding stone, allowing the viewer to see through the sculpture. Open form can exist in both naturalistic and abstract sculpture. Often the points of extension can be a point of weakness in the form, hence the large quantity of Greek and Roman sculptures with broken arms or missing hands or heads.

This Mayan sculpture from the late classic period (AD 550–830) is an excellent example of the use of mass in a three-dimensional sculpture (Figure 2.2). ***Mass***, in art as in science, is the combination of volume and density. Volume, then, is shape in three dimensions, and density is the actual or perceived weight of an object. While you may have a cube filled with feathers or a cube filled with lead, they both have volume, but the cube filled with lead has more mass.

In terms of art, mass and form are used somewhat interchangeably. Some sculptures, such as this sculpture of a Mayan man (see Figure 2.2), are said to be open form. Open form is when an object is freestanding

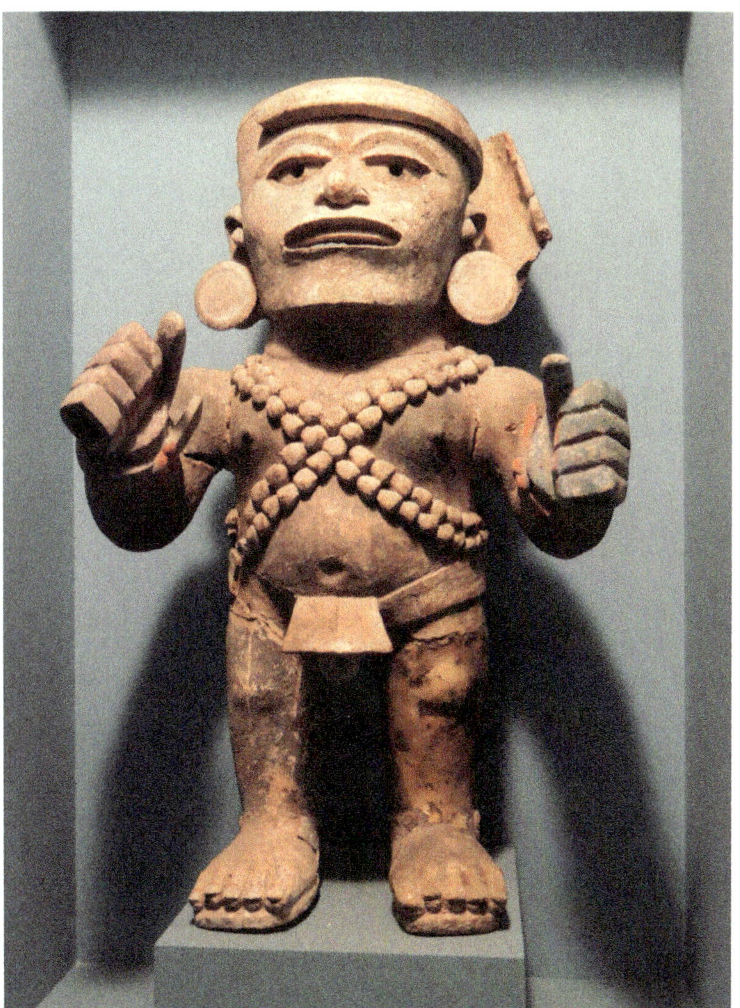

FIG. 2.2 Mayan sculpture, Late Classic Period. Example of mass.Copyright in the Public Domain.

and not attached to the material from which it was created. The space between the legs and the space between the arms and the body of the man are absent, whereas in closed form the clay would still be present. This lends solidity to the form but makes it seem more rigid and formal. This sculpture, being open form, has life-likeness to it that closed form often lacks.

The Guanyin Buddha is located in the Tower of Buddhist Incense in the Summer Palace. The Buddha was cast in bronze in 1574 and stands just shy of 16 ½ feet tall (Figure 2.3). The sculpture is gilded and has a head of four tiers, each with three faces, for a total of twelve faces and twenty-four arms. The statue is seated on a lotus set of nine layers and nine hundred ninety nine petals. This sculpture, with its gracefully waving arms, is an excellent example of open form.

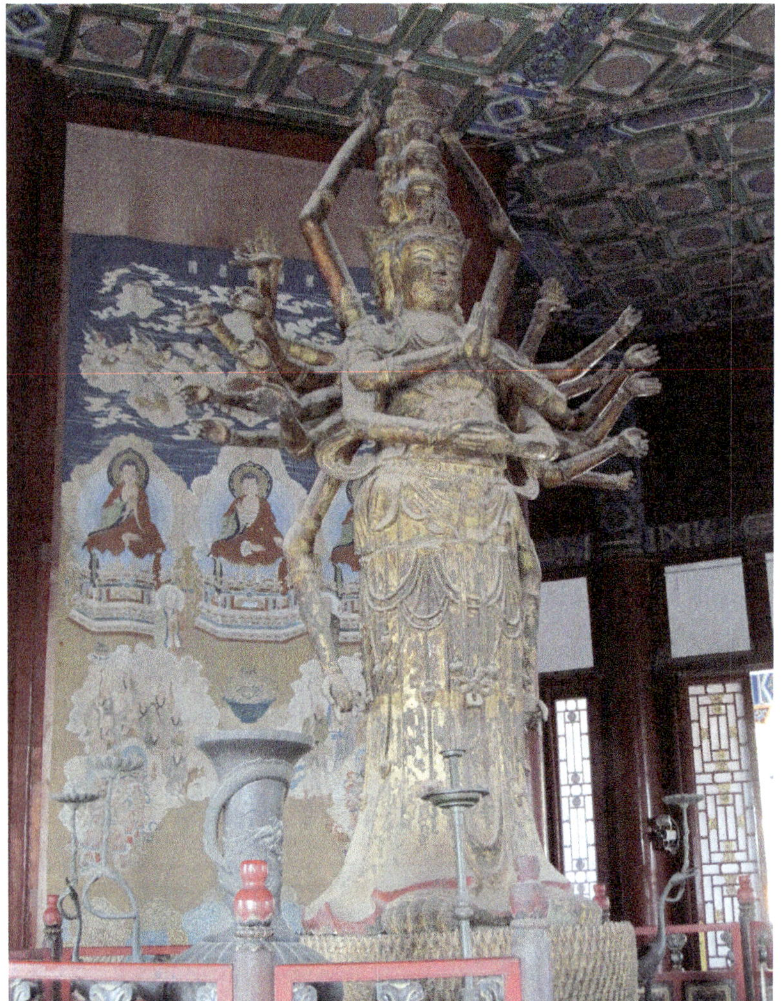

FIG. 2.3 Guanyin Statue in the Summer Palace. Example of open form

Closed form, like the type of form commonly produced by the Egyptians, is made without any visible openings. The place where there should logically be an opening, such as when an arm rests at one's side, is still attached to the stone from which it was carved. This allows for greater strength in the overall sculpture, since gaps in the piece would be a natural weak spot where breakage is more likely. Closed form is a very sturdy, solidly constructed type of sculpture.

Isis is the Egyptian goddess connected to the rites of the dead and is often seen as the female counterpart to Osiris. Isis is traditionally depicted as a beautiful woman wearing a sheath dress with the hieroglyphic sign of the throne (which represents her name) on a solar disk and a cow's horns on her head. Isis is sometimes depicted with wings. She was married to her brother Osiris (the judge of the dead) and is the mother of Horus (the god of Light). She is often seen as a role model for women or as the mother-goddess (Tyldesley). This sculpture is obviously missing its head (Figure 2.4),

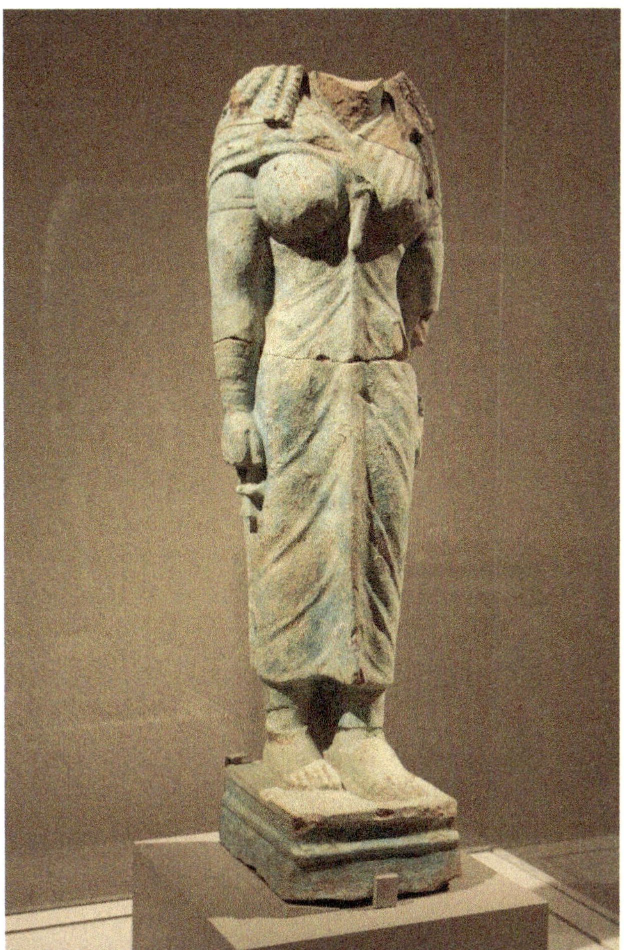

FIG. 2.4 Statue of Isis. Example of closed form. Copyright © Sven-Steffen Arndt (CC BY-SA 2.0) at https://commons.wikimedia.org/wiki/File:Aegyptisches_Museum_Berlin_InvNrKA_20080313_Goettin_Isis_aus_Naga.jpg.

but there is more than enough remaining to identify which goddess she is meant to be. This is a good example of the type of closed form favored by the Egyptians. Notice the space between the feet, which should be open so that the viewer can see between the feet, is still attached to the stone from which it was carved. The same is true of the space between the elbow and the side of Isis's body. She is standing in the classic Egyptian pose with the left foot forward and the arms tight at the sides.

PROJECT IDEAS

Geometric v. Organic

Geometric shapes are precise and regular and encompass such things as triangles, circles, and squares. Organic shapes are irregular and are often seen as more relaxed compared to geometric shapes. Create a drawing of an organic object on one half of the paper. On the other half of the paper draw the same object using only geometric shapes. An example of this would be a drawing of an orange on one side of the paper and a perfect circle on the other side of the paper.

Overlapping Forms

Overlapping one object in front of another can create the illusion of depth in an image. Using cut paper shapes, demonstrate the concept of overlapping by gluing the shapes down in such a way that the overlap is clearly visible to the viewer.

Vertical Placement

Vertical placement is used to create the idea that an object is in front of similar objects. This concept is created by placing objects closer to the bottom of the image and making them larger than the objects closer to the middle or top of the image. Using a series of similar objects in varying sizes (such as a row of oranges) create an image that uses vertical placement to imply that one of the objects is closer to the viewer than the other objects.

Chapter 3
Light and Color

DEFINITION AND TYPES

Light is a type of radiant energy that we have learned to simulate using electricity (Getlein). Artists often use both implied and actual light in the creation of their works. (According to Lucy Lamp, "Light in art includes using actual light—the lighting of artwork, how a light source might interact with an artwork, the use of reflections, and using light itself as an artistic medium—as well as using implied light to create the illusion of light in two-dimensional work" (Lamp).

In a two-dimensional composition, ***light*** is implied since the actual application of light has to be painted or drawn onto the surface. Light can be used to expose color, such as in the work of the Impressionist painters, or to expose a delicate surface or texture. Viewers are often able to identify a strong light source in a painting or drawing but struggle with finding the light source when it is more subtle.

Chiaroscuro is an Italian term that literally means bright (chiaro)/dark (oscuro) and is the distribution of light and dark within a composition. Getlein (2012) notes that, "with chiaroscuro, artists employ values—lights and darks—to record contrasts of light and shdow in the natural world, contrasts that model mass for our eyes" (pp. 88). The lighting of a work of art in a gallery would be actual light and can greatly impact the way the viewer sees the work of art. Lighting is an important facet of hanging a show or displaying a sculptural form to its greatest advantage.

Spectrum v. Pigment

The ***light spectrum***, as discovered by Sir Isaac Newton in 1672, uses light reflected through a prism to divide white light into its separate components of red, orange, yellow, green, blue, indigo, and violet. The spectrum is pure light and, consequently, pure color. The artist's color wheel is a tool used by artists that simulates the colors found in the spectrum but eliminates indigo as it is generally replaced by blue-violet in most color theories.

Pigment, on the other hand, is any form of powder coloring agents that are used to create approximations of the colors found in the spectrum. Pigment can be made of substances either natural or chemical, such as shell, earth, grasses, ground stone, bug shells, organic plant materials, or foodstuffs. Today, most pigment is chemically simulated as opposed to natural pigments. Pigment is used as a coloring agent in all drawing media, paint, and glaze, although with glaze the chemical process changes during firing. The color names of various pigments, such as red-orange or blue, are known as ***hue***.

Value and Intensity

Value is the relative lightness or darkness of a color or hue. This property of color tells us how light or dark a color is based on how close it is to white (Figure 3.1). Yellow, for example, is the lightest color on the color wheel, while its compliment, violet, is the darkest value on the color wheel.

Intensity or ***Saturation*** refers to the relative purity of a color or hue (Figure 3.2). This property of color tells us how bright or dull a color is. The brightest intensity would be a color that is totally pure and not dulled with the addtion of any other color. Colors can be dulled until they appear gray, traditionally by mixing the color with its complement. An example of a high intensity color would be highlighter yellow, while mustard yellow would be considered low intensity.

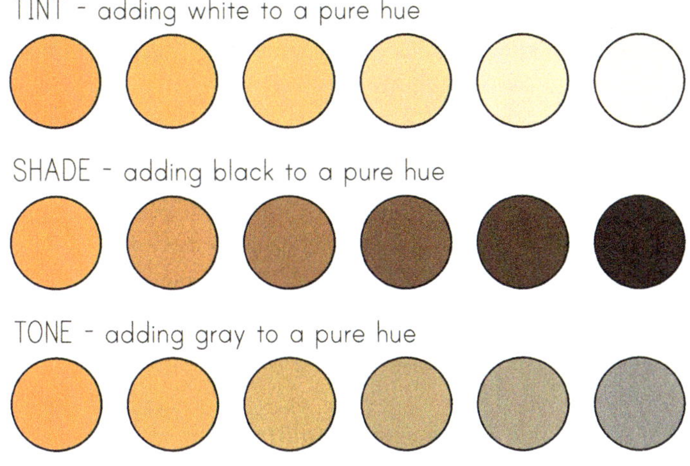

FIG. 3.1 Tint, shade, and tone.

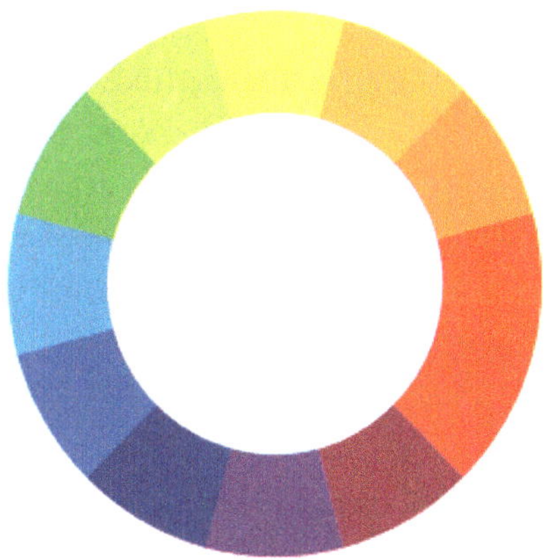

FIG. 3.2 Color wheel. Copyright © Sakurambo (CC BY-SA 3.0) at https://commons.wikimedia.org/wiki/File%3ABYR_color_wheel.svg.

Color Systems

There are many different color systems designed to help artists and designers use color effectively in their work. Louis Prang, a prominent lithographer from the Boston area developed a series of color theories from which a color wheel was developed in 1876.

To read more about Prang's theories, please see this website: http://www.examiner.com/article/the-color-wheel-and-color-theory-important-tools-for-interior-design; http://www.uwgb.edu/heuerc/2d/colorsystm.html.

This color system is referred to as the Prang or Artist's color system. The Prang or Artist color system separates the twelve basic colors of the color wheel into ***primary***, ***secondary*** and ***tertiary*** colors. There are several other color systems in use—most notably CMYK—that combine the colors in other ways, but the Prang system is the one most often taught in public schools.

CMYK, or the four-color system, is most often used in the printing industry. CMYK separates the four basic colors from which every other color can be mixed into **c**yan, **m**agenta, **y**ellow, and blac**k.** Other colors systems include Munsell, Ostwald, Schopenhauer, subtractive color, and RGB or additive color.

In the Prang color system, ***primary colors*** are those colors that cannot be created by combining colors on the color wheel. The primary colors are red, yellow, and blue. ***Secondary colors*** are those colors that are created by combining the primary colors that are adjacent to one another on the color wheel. Green (blue + yellow), orange (red + yellow), and violet (red + blue) are the secondary colors. ***Tertiary colors*** are those colors that are created by combining a primary and a secondary color. These colors are easily identified by their two word color names. Yellow-green, yellow-orange, red-orange, red-violet, blue-violet, and blue-green are the tertiary colors.

Color Schemes

Monochromatic color schemes use one color plus tints and shades of that color to achieve an extremely unified look in a composition. Often there may be small touches of other colors in the composition, but if the dominant color scheme uses one color, it is still considered to be monochromatic.

Rocks at Night by Paul Klee (Figure 3.3) is a fine example of the use of monochromatic color in a composition. A ***monochromatic color*** scheme uses one color plus tints and shades of that color as the primary colors in the composition. In this case, Klee has created a true monochromatic composition, but other artists may incorporate a small selection of other colors and still have the image considered monochromatic as long as the overall color scheme is dominated by one color. Klee's use of blue and shades and tints of blue create the feeling of a nighttime scene in this abstracted image.

Analogous color schemes use colors that are adjacent on the color wheel. These colors are seen as especially harmonious as they usually

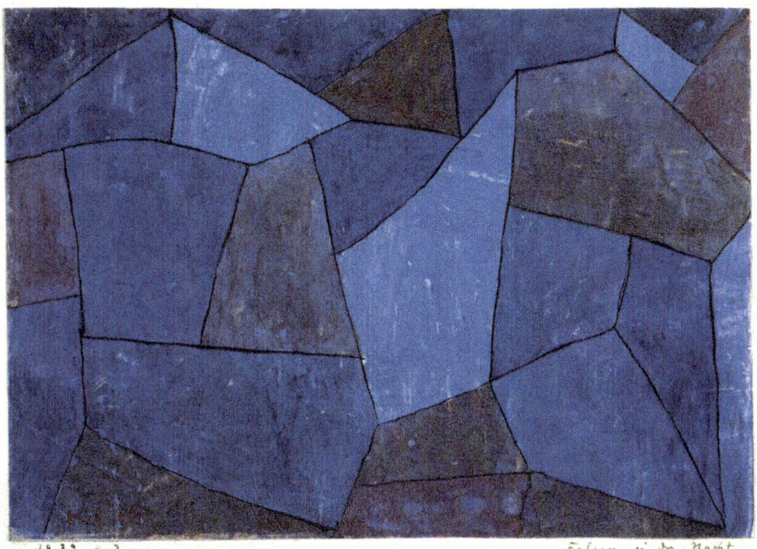

FIG. 3.3 Monochromatic color. Paul Klee, Rocks at Night, 1939. Watercolor and ink on chalk- and glue-primed letter paper, mounted on paper, 20.9 × 29.5 cm. Solomon R. Guggenheim Museum, New York. Copyright © 2015 Artists Rights Society (ARS), New York / VG Bild-Kunst, Bonn.

have the same base color. Yellow-green, green, and blue-green make an analogous color scheme (Figure 3.4).

Bend in the Road by Paul Cezanne (see next page) uses an analogous color scheme to achieve visual harmony in this simple landscape. An

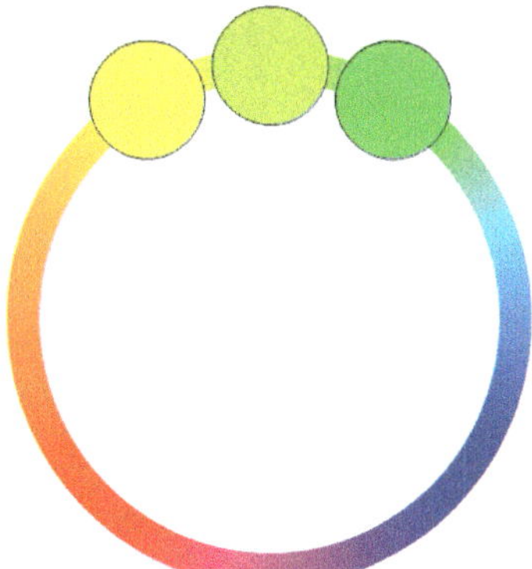

FIG. 3.4 Analogous color wheel. Copyright © Trond Grøntoft (CC BY-SA 3.0) at https://commons.wikimedia.org/wiki/File%3AAnalogousColors.png.

analogous color scheme features three colors that are adjacent to each other on the color wheel. In this case the colors are blue, blue-green, and green, with tints and shades of each color. Analogous color schemes are seen as low contrast since each color is so close to the others on the color wheel. Cezanne's use of small bits of red and orange in the image are striking in their contrast to the blue-green palette of the rest of image in both the complimentary nature of blue and orange and in the warm temperature of the red-orange color against the cool temperature of the blues that dominate the overall composition (Figure 3.5).

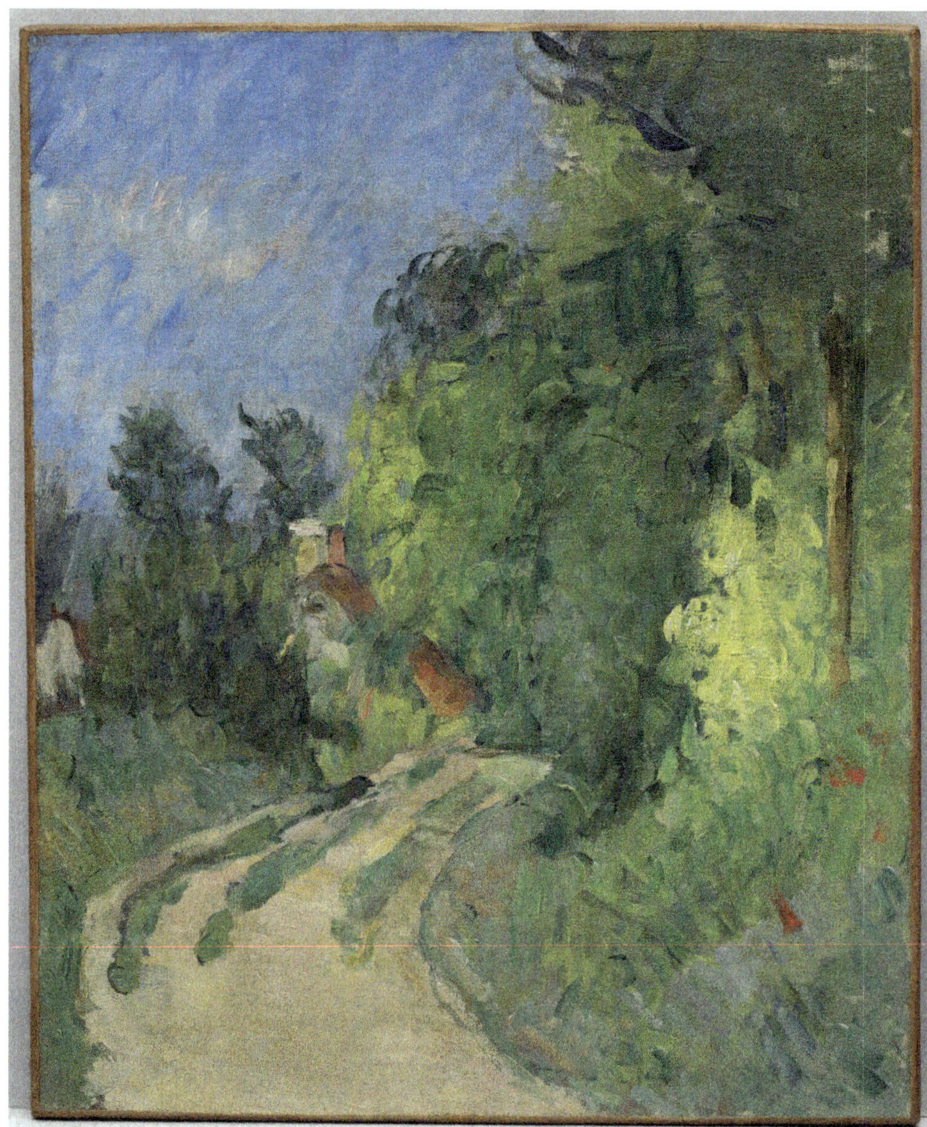

FIG. 3.5 Analogous color. Paul Cézanne, Bend in the Road Through the Forest, 1873-1875. Oil on canvas, 55 × 46 cm. Solomon R. Guggenheim Museum, New York. Copyright in the Public Domain.

Complimentary color schemes use colors that are opposites on the color wheel. This type of color scheme is high contrast and is often used when an artist wants something to stand out in his or her work. Red and green, blue and orange, and yellow and violet are complimentary color schemes (Figure 3.6).

Fatigue by Ramon Casas features a woman with her head pillowed on her arms leaning on a tabletop. The bright green of the table and chair contrasts highly with the use of varying shades of red in the background of the image. ***Complimentary colors***, such as the red and green used predominantly in this image, are opposites on the color wheel and provide strong contrast when used in proximity of each other in a composition.

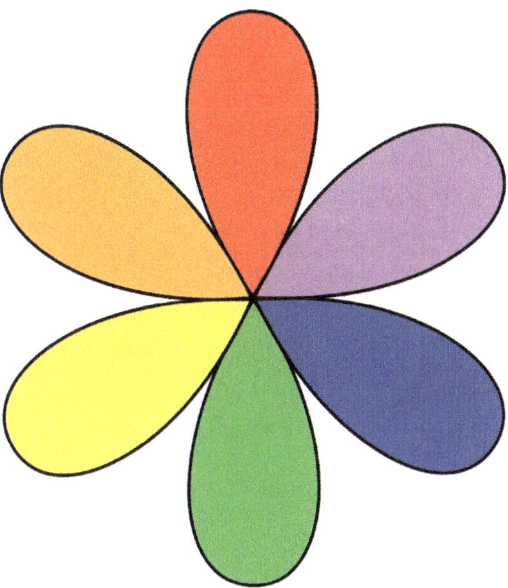

FIG. 3.6 Complimentary color wheel. Copyright in the Public Domain.

Even the woman, with her reddish skin tone and gown with its green highlights, plays into the overall color scheme (Figure 3.7).

Triadic color schemes use colors that are equidistant on the color wheel. Triadic color schemes are usually quite vibrant due to the high-contrast nature of the colors being so separate from one another on the color wheel. Violet, orange, and green, in addition to being the secondary colors, are also a triadic color scheme.

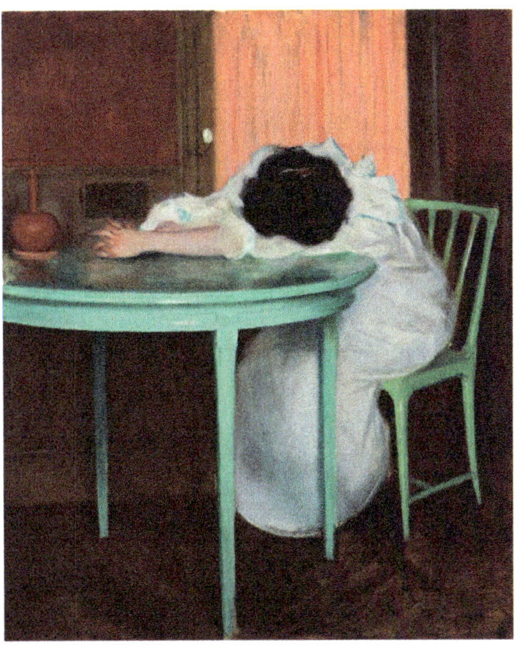

FIG. 3.7 Complimentary colors. Ramon Casas, Tired, 1895-1900. Oil on canvas, 96.2 × 85.41 × 7.3 cm. Dallas Museum of Art. Copyright in the Public Domain.

Color Temperature

Warm colors are those colors on the color wheel that are reminiscent of fire, heat, or warmth. Warm colors are yellow, yellow-orange, orange, red-orange, and red. Yellow-green and red-violet can be seen as either warm or cool depending on what other colors they are paired with in a composition. Warm colors seem to advance in space when used in a work of art.

Cool colors are those colors on the color wheel that are reminiscent of water, ice, or freshness. Cool colors include green, blue-green, blue, blue-violet, and violet. Yellow-green and red-violet can be seen as either warm or cool depending on what other colors they are paired with in a composition. Cool colors seem to recede in space when used in a work of art.

PROJECT IDEAS

Color Wheel

A color wheel is a tool used by artists to organize hue into primary, secondary, and tertiary colors. Additionally, a color wheel can be used to define color relationships such as complementary, analogous, and split-complementary hues. Create a color wheel by dividing a circle into twelve equal parts. Place the primary colors around the circle leaving three spaces in between each primary color. Place the appropriate secondary colors in the middle space between each primary color. The tertiary colors should be placed beside their corresponding secondary colors. Label each color after you have filled in the circle in the correct order.

Value Scale

A value scale is a tool used by artists to define changes in a hue from lightest (white) to darkest (black). Place the pure hue in the center of a two-inch wide strip that has been divided into seven equal sections. Place the black square at one end of the strip and the white square at the other end of the strip. Beginning with the pure hue, mix two shades of the color using black. Paint each of the squares between the hue square and the black square, with the darker color being placed closest to the black square. Repeat this procedure with white and the pure hue, creating tints of the original color with the lightest color placed closer to the white square. A value scale can have any number of squares between the hue, black, and white squares depending on how in-depth you wish the color scale to be.

Intensity

Color intensity is the degree to which a hue appears its brightest or lightest. To change the intensity of a hue, on a color wheel find where yellow is and look for the purple on the other side. (Any complementary color pair will work.) Mix the two complementary colors together and add white to the mixture. This will make the yellow darker and thus will make the yellow less intense.

Experiment by changing the intensity of two hues from the color wheel by mixing the hues with their complements plus white.

Chapter 4
Space

DEFINITION AND TYPES

Space

In three dimensions, ***space*** is found in architecture and sculpture. Architecture is enclosed space although it also interacts with the space around the building itself. The building then serves as the ***positive space*** while the space around the building functions as the ***negative space***. Positive and negative space occurs in two-dimensional compositions as well although the effect is simulated since any type of depth in two dimensions is always simulated.

Techniques for Creating Perceptions of Depth

There are several ways to simulate the effect of depth on a two-dimensional surface. Overlapping, diminishing size, and vertical placement are three such ways to simulate depth. In ***overlapping,*** the artist draws objects as if they are sitting one in front of the other by removing the portions of the object meant to be "behind" the object in front so that it appears to be in front of the object behind. For example, if I am drawing a row of spheres, and I want them to overlap, then I will draw one sphere in its entirety, and each succeeding sphere will be partially covered by the sphere next to it. The effect is one of a row of spheres that overlap.

Overlapping is one of the ways artists create a sense of space on a two-dimensional surface. In *The Puppet Play* by Genshi Kyoraishi (Figure 4.1) space is created using overlapping and one-point perspective. The vanishing point is clearly visible, and all of the orthogonal lines on both the floor and the ceiling of the room lead the viewer directly to the window in the back of the room, creating a sense of deep space. The artist uses diminishing size to increase the sense of space as well with each group of people watching the play decreasing in size as they approach the horizon line.

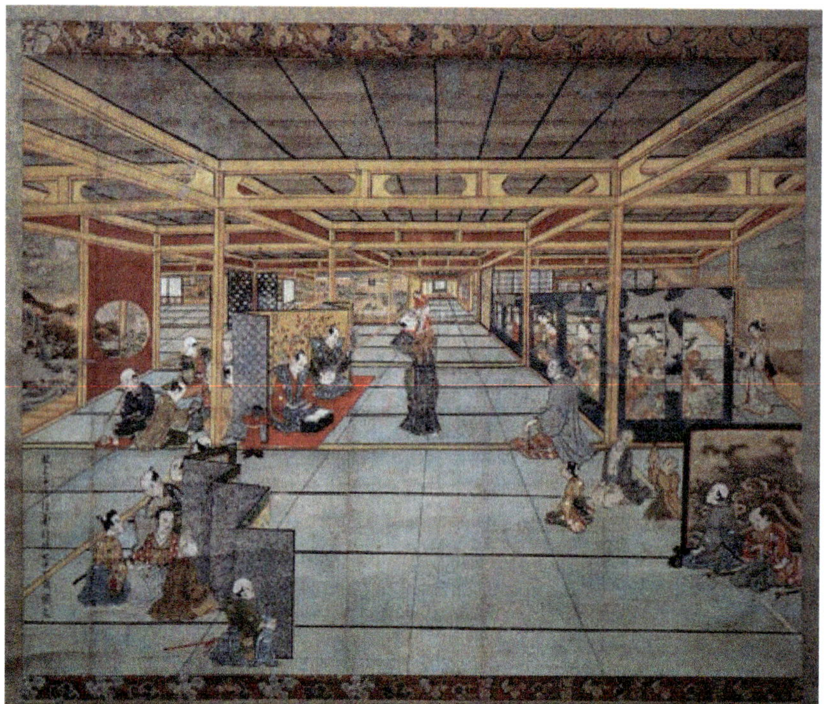

FIG. 4.1 Linear perspective. Genshin Kyoraishi, The Puppet Play in a Teahouse. Ink and watercolor on paper, 64.6 × 84.5 cm. National Museum in Warsaw. Copyright in the Public Domain.

In ***diminishing size,*** the artist makes objects appear further in the distance by reducing the size of objects as they move toward the top of the composition as the viewer has a tendency to view the bottom of the composition as closer and the top of the composition as farther away. Reducing the size of objects as they approach the top of the composition enhances the illusion. In ***vertical placement,*** the artist makes objects appear as if they are closer by placing them toward the bottom of the composition. For example, if I draw a row of spheres and draw one of them below the row it will appear "closer" to the viewer. Using diminishing size in conjunction with vertical placement can reinforce this illusion of depth.

Establishing a clear foreground, middle ground, and background can help with the illusion of depth in a composition. ***Foreground*** is the area in a composition that is meant to appear closest to the viewer while the ***background*** is meant to appear as the farthest away from the viewer while the ***middle ground*** is the area between the foreground and background.

Perspective incorporates some or all of the above strategies for achieving the illusion of depth in a two-dimensional composition. Perspective, then, is any means of creating three-dimensional depth on a two-dimensional surface. There are several types of perspective: linear, atmospheric or aerial, and isometric.

Linear perspective was fully developed during the Italian Renaissance by the architect Filippo Brunelleschi beginning in about 1415 (Blumberg) following his attempts to paint the Baptistry of the Florence Cathedral as it appeared to his eye. Brunelleschi's success in the development of linear perspective came after several earlier artists used rudimentary systems of perspective in their work. In fact, use of simple perspective systems are found in early Greek and Roman works although those systems did not have the mathematical perfection of true linear perspective.

Linear perspective begins with a horizon line and includes one or more vanishing points and orthogonal (parallel lines) which help define the foreground and background of the composition. The ***horizon line*** is the point in the composition where the land and sky appear to meet. The horizon point also represents the ***eye level*** of the viewer as he or she looks at the scene. The ***vanishing point*** is the point on the horizon where the ***orthogonal lines*** converge. Imagine driving on a tree-lined interstate with nothing impeding the view of the horizon. The point where the road seems to disappear into the distance is the vanishing point. The straight lines of the road are the orthogonals and help define the foreground of the composition (Figure 4.2, page 28).

In this photograph the artist has created an excellent example of one-point perspective. The road seems to converge at the horizon line that is clearly visible due to the lack of vegetation along the road. The mountains in the distance provide a sense of deep space and appear to become progressively hazy-blue in color until they seem to merge with the blue of the sky. The horizon line and vanishing point are very easy to pick out in this example as are the orthogonal lines provided by the lines on the road and the sand on either side of the pavement.

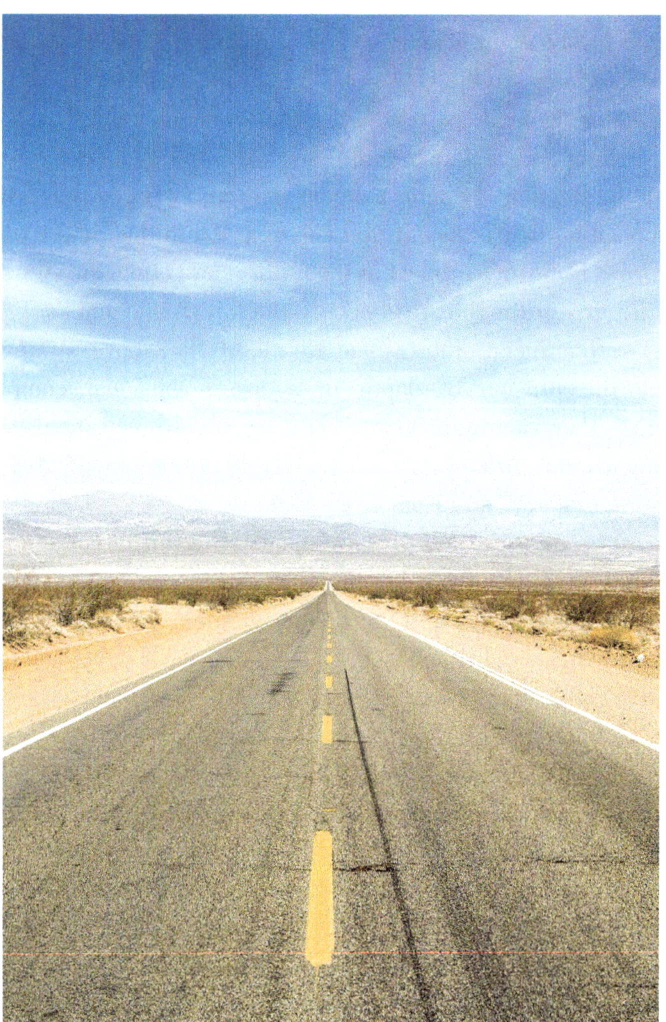

FIG. 4.2 *The Road Ahead.* One-point perspective. Copyright © russavia (CC BY-SA 2.0) at https://commons.wikimedia.org/wiki/File:The_road_ahead_(2046262670).jpg.

While traditional ***one-point perspective*** has a single vanishing point, there are other types of linear perspective that have multiple vanishing points. In ***two-point perspective***, for example, there are two vanishing points created by using two sets of orthogonal lines converging at two points on the horizon. Imagine yourself standing at the intersection of two roads. Looking in either direction you can see two points on the horizon; that is two-point perspective.

Atmospheric or aerial perspective is a type of perspective that uses changes in color, value, and detail to achieve a sense of deep space within a composition. This type of perspective is non-linear. Similar to viewing an object from a distance, atmospheric perspective makes use of the idea that as objects recede into the distance, they become gray and indistinct. Color intensity is greatly diminished, and contrast is softened to help the illusion of great distance. Sharpening the objects in the foreground and placing objects in the middle ground help the illusion, as does the use of diminishing size within the composition (Figure 4.3).

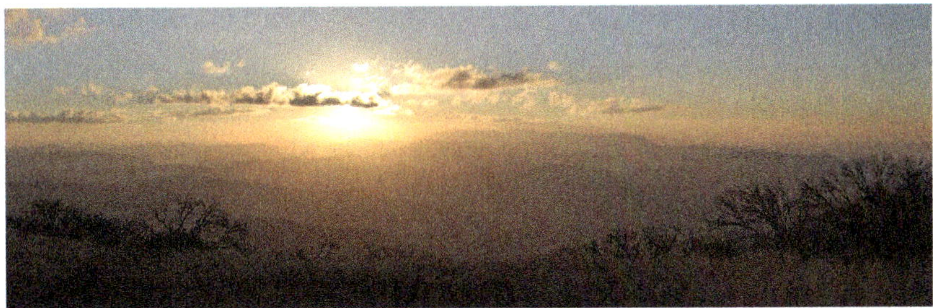

FIG. 4.3 Mount Feathertop, Alpine Victoria, Australia. Atmospheric perspective. Copyright © Diliff (CC BY-SA 3.0) at https://commons.wikimedia.org/wiki/File:Mount_Feathertop,_Australia_-_May_2005.jpg.

Mount Feathertop, the second-highest mountain in the Australian Alps in the state of Victoria, provides the backdrop for this example of atmospheric perspective. The photographer catches the view at sunset from the summit of the mountain, creating a strongly horizontal composition with mountains disappearing into the golden glow of the sunset in the distance. The trees are in the foreground while the mountains get progressively smaller as they approach the horizon in the background. The clouds provide a middle ground that adds to the drama of this photograph.

Isometric perspective is often seen in the creation of computer graphics and games. Isometric perspective is a type of perspective that eliminates the distortion of shape created by true perspective. In isometric perspective all lines on each axis are parallel to one another and do not converge on a horizon line like in linear perspective. Isometric perspective is meant to show objects with as much detail as possible and as such is often used for technical drawings and diagrams.

PROJECT IDEAS

Linear Perspective

Linear perspective is a system designed to simulate the look of objects going back in space on a flat two-dimensional picture plane. To create the classic example of linear perspective (that of a road going into the distance) draw a line horizontally across the page to represent the horizon line. Starting at the bottom of the page draw a line that angles slightly and ends at the horizon line. Add a second line that begins at the bottom of the page and angles toward the first line. This will create the illusion of a road disappearing into the distance. The illusion can be enhanced by adding lines on the road that get smaller as they approach the horizon line, trees along the edge of the road that also decrease in size, and clouds in the sky.

Atmospheric Perspective

Atmospheric perspective is a type of perspective that creates the illusion of deep space by blurring the images as they recede into the distance. The use of hazy, indistinct color adds to the illusion of deep space. To create an example of atmospheric perspective (looking at mountains in the distance) draw an object in the foreground of the paper. This object should be as detailed as you can draw it. Draw a series of trees on hills in the mid-ground of the image that are smaller than the detailed image in the foreground (i.e., still green for the leaves but no distinct leaves on the trees). In the background draw a series of smaller hills, but when adding the color, make the color a hazy blue -gray. Adding additional objects to the scene, such as birds in the mid-ground, will add to the illusion of deep space.

Chapter 5

Time and Motion

DEFINITION AND TYPES

Portrayals of Movement and Time

Actual or ***kinetic motion*** is exactly as it sounds: the physical movement of a work of art. This movement can be either natural or manmade. Natural movement would be environmental while manmade movement usually involves the use of motors. ***Implied motion*** is the act of simulating movement on a two-dimensional picture plane. This can be accomplished through the use of subject matter or through the use of paint or pencil application on the surface of the work.

In *The Cyclist* by Natalia Goncharova the artist is implying motion by making the primary image, that of a cyclist on a bicycle, appear in multiples. Slightly overlapping, these multiples give the impression that the cyclist is moving forward on his bicycle. The fact that the background and ground under the bicycle is not moving is meant to enhance the illusion of movement. The effect is similar to that of a strobe light, where movement is seen as a type of aura that extends behind the figure as it moves through space (Figure 5.1, page 32).

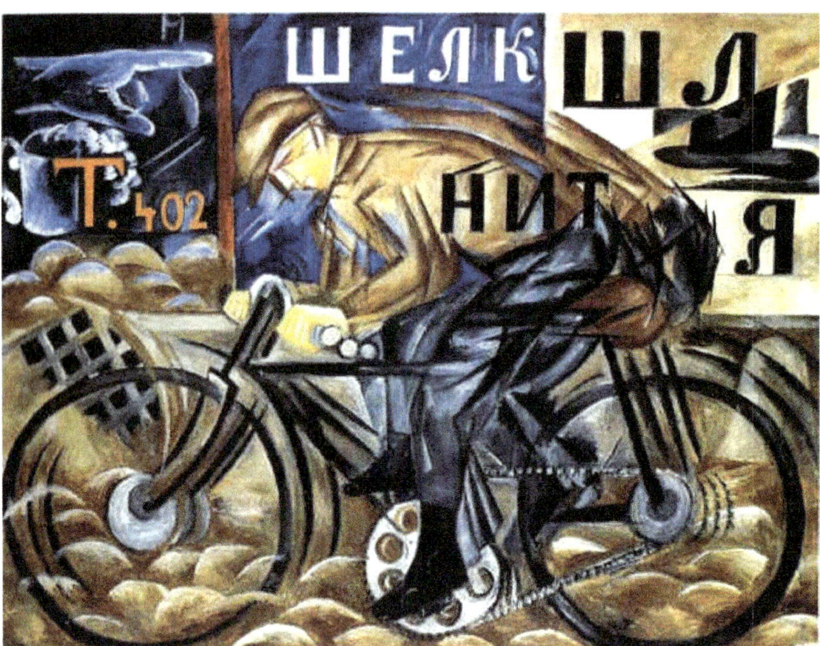

FIG. 5.1 Motion. Natalia Goncharova, The Cyclist. The Russian Museum, St. Petersburg. Oil on canvas, 78 × 105 cm. Copyright in the Public Domain.

Time is much more difficult to portray on a two-dimensional surface, and artists throughout time have tried to solve the problem in a variety of ways. One of those ways is to create vignettes depicting different moments in the timeline of the subject all within the same composition. This would be similar to a picture in a picture on a television set. This technique presupposes that the viewer is familiar with the story being depicted in the composition and can follow the multiple storylines being presented on the canvas. Another technique would be to use a graphic-novel or comic-strip approach where the different scenes are depicted as appearing in chronological order in successive panels. This technique can be quite effective in showing the passage of time.

In the comic strip *Dennisisms* created by Dennis Johnson, the artist has shown the movement of time in a series of panels. Each panel is a distinct scene, and together they form a continuous whole. By framing each panel as a moment in an overall event, the panels function both independently and as part of a larger whole (Figure 5.2).

Film and ***video*** show the actual passage of time although it is often what is referred to as manipulated time. ***Manipulated time*** is edited to allow a series of events happening over a large span of time to be condensed into a shortened time frame. A movie, for example, is a good example of manipulated time, where a person's entire life might take place in two hours. In a true motion picture camera, unlike a more contemporary

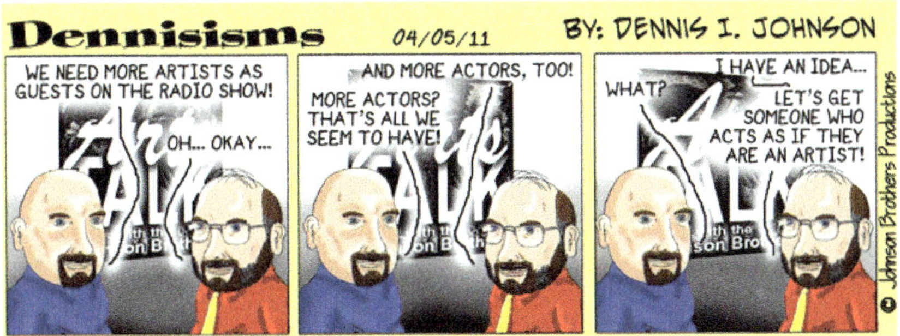

FIG. 5.2 Time. Dennis I. Johnson, "Dennisims 04/05/11." Copyright in the Public Domain.

digital camera, the film is literally set in motion just fast enough that the human eye cannot see the individual still images, and the final effect is of a smooth, unbroken string of images each one flowing into the next.

PROJECT IDEAS

Sequential Art (Comic Strips)

A comic strip is a basic type of sequential art. Flipbooks, video, and film are also types of sequential art. To create a three-panel comic strip, first divide the paper into three equal sections. Draw a square in each section. These squares should be equal in size. Decide on a basic character for your comic. Create a short story for your character. This story should be easily resolved in three panels. Sketch your story into the three squares. Add thought bubbles for the dialogue. Sketch in the dialogue neatly—if no one can read your hand lettering, it is pointless to have dialogue. Using a permanent marker, neatly trace over your sketched lines and dialogue. Trace around the squares you created for the comic panels. You may choose to add color to enhance your design.

Repetition of Form

One of the ways an artist shows movement is through the repetition of form. A classic example is the Futurist painting *Dynamism of a Dog on a Leash* (1912) by Giacomo Balla. To create this effect, first draw a simple object that moves. It can be an organic (living) object such as an animal or inorganic (non-living) object such as a car. Once the object is drawn, you can add multiples of the moving parts, like the dog's tail in the Balla painting. By staggering the moving parts slightly, you can make the drawing look as if it is in motion. The key to this drawing is to make the original part of the moving object less detailed because it will make the repetition of the object easier to execute.

Flipbooks

A flipbook is usually a small book with multiple pages. Flipbooks are used to show the sequential movement of an object, such as a ball rolling down a hill, and are considered a basic animation technique. To create a flipbook, take a piece of typing paper and cut it into fifteen to twenty equal-size pieces. Thin paper works better for this technique, as thicker paper will make the flipbook look jerky. Stack the pieces of paper together and use a clip to hold them in place. Draw a simple object on the bottom sheet of paper. For each subsequent page, draw the same object in a very slightly different position using the drawing underneath as a reference. If the drawing on the page underneath does not show through well, go over the drawing with pencil to make it darker. If you are drawing a static object such as a house, you can create the idea of movement through the sun moving in the sky or curtains moving in the windows. Once all of the drawings are in place, simply flip through the pages to see your object move.

Chapter 6

Texture

DEFINITION AND TYPES

Texture is the tactile (touchable) quality of an object. Texture is a fairly straightforward concept because the average person already has a large collection of textures memorized. We draw from these memories when we look at a work of art, and they help inform our awareness of the world around us. Texture is found in the cool, smooth feel of metal versus the roughness of sandpaper, the feel of a plastic bottle versus wood, or cotton balls versus tree bark, the feel of fur versus leather. Artists often try to either use or recreate these textures in their works.

Actual texture is texture that can be touched. It can be found in the use of varying types of stone in a sculpture or fur on a teacup. Three-dimensional artwork is made up of texture, even if we as the viewer are not actually allowed to touch the work in question.

Taos Mountain Trail by Cordelia Wilson is a good example of ***actual texture*** used in a painting. Wilson uses a thickened form of oil paint to create a texture that is evident when the painting is viewed up close. This abstract image of a group of people on horseback approaching the mountains in the distance is enhanced through the use of this type of painting technique, which adds visual interest in a painting with a fairly muted color palette (Figure 6.1).

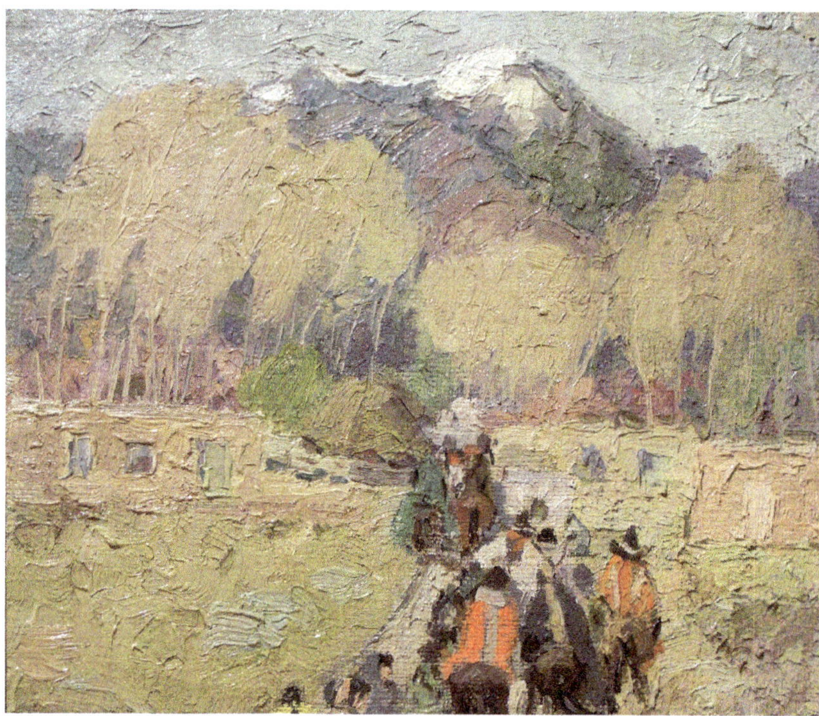

FIG. 6.1 Actual texture. Cordelia Wilson, Taos Mountain, Trail Home, 1915-1920s. Oil painting. Copyright in the Public Domain.

Implied texture is the act of simulating actual texture on a two-dimensional surface. To recreate the look of fur, for example, would be an implied texture for although it looks like fur, it is not actually fur. Some artists create two-dimensional work that incorporates different actual textures into the composition (Figure 6.2).

The Merchant Georg Gisze by Hans Holbein the Younger contains a number of different ***implied textures*** within the image. The differences between the types of smooth fabric in the textiles contrast with the roughness of the paneling behind the man. Various implements sitting on the table, each made to mimic a different material, are a masterwork of the use of implied texture, creating an image that is full of iconography and forms a visual biography of Georg Gisze, a merchant Holbein painted in London in 1532. Holbein was well known for his depiction of both objects and textures as is evidenced in this work.

Trompe l'oeil is a French term that means "to fool the eye" and refers to a type of painting or drawing that is so super realistic that it tricks the viewer into thinking it is real. Artists often use appropriate scale to enhance the illusion of reality in this type of work.

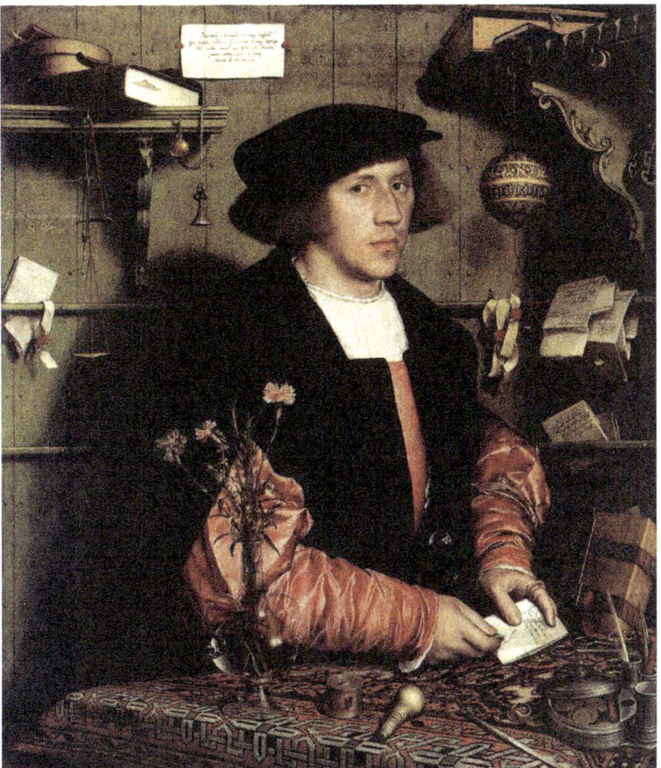

FIG. 6.2 Texture. Hans Holbein the Younger, The Merchant Georg Gisze, 1532. Oil on oak. 86.2 × 97.5 cm. Copyright in the Public Domain.

PROJECT IDEAS

Implied Texture Grid

Texture is the tactile (touchable) aspect of an object. Texture can be smooth, rough, soft, hard, scratchy, slick etc. Texture in art can be either implied or actual. An actual texture can be seen in many multi-media works in which a variety of materials are used to complete the artwork. Implied texture is present in a work when an artist simulates the look of a texture. A painting of an animal may look like fur but not actually feel like fur when touched. To create an implied texture, you should look at the object you are trying to simulate. Divide a piece of paper into six even squares and draw a texture into each square. Make sure to label each texture. Color can be an excellent way to help show an implied texture.

Actual Texture Grid

To create an actual texture grid divide your paper into six equal squares. Collect a variety of objects with different textures. An example of an actual texture would be sandpaper, which has a scratchy texture. Cut each object to fit into one of the squares on your paper. Attach your objects to your paper using glue or tape. Make sure the objects are securely fastened to the paper. Make sure to label each texture neatly.

Creating Simulated Texture

Executing a rubbing can be a good way to create a simulated texture. An example of a rubbing would be to place a piece of corrugated cardboard under your paper and use your pencil to rub over the paper which will transfer the texture of the cardboard onto the paper. Divide your paper into three squares, and using the rubbing technique show three different textures. Make sure to label each texture neatly.

Chapter 7

The Principles of Design: Unity and Variety

DEFINITION AND TYPES

Unity is the appearance or condition of oneness in a composition. In an artwork, unity occurs when the objects, colors, forms, and/or subject of the work appear to be in harmony with one another without any one thing in the composition standing out as being out of place. If, for example, the artist painted a meadow with cows and a babbling brook, unity would occur because the scale, color, and form of those objects make sense to the viewer. If the artist then painted a skyscraper in the middle of the meadow, unity would be affected because there would be no logical reason for a skyscraper to exist in the middle of a meadow with cows. That is an extreme example, but unity is a concept that is usually readily apparent to the viewer. Certain art movements, such as surrealism, play with the concept of unity, often adding elements to works that seem out of place in order to keep the viewer off-balance when viewing the work.

In *Three Beeches* by Paul Ranson, the artist has created a unified composition that provides enough variety to be interesting. The unity is provided by a color palette that is similar from tree to tree. The brush stroke is similar throughout the entire composition as is the color. There is nothing in the composition that truly stands out, and thus the viewer would consider this a very unified composition. The variety comes in the subtle differences between each of the trees, the differences in diameter of each tree, the amount of moss on each tree, and the subtle color differences. Overall this composition would be considered very unified in that there isn't anything that stands out as being an anomaly (Figure 7.1).

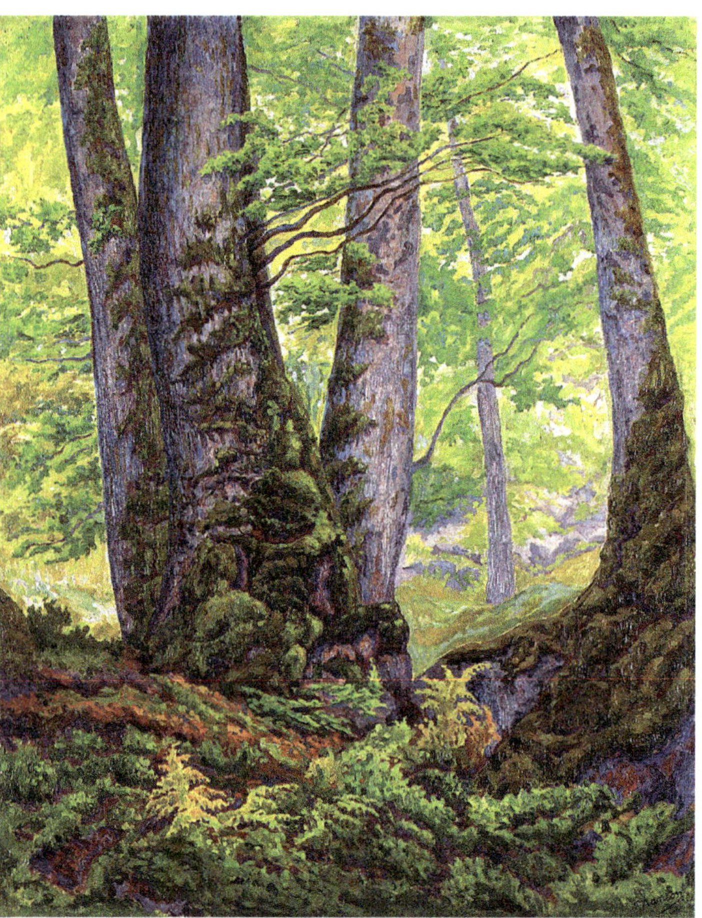

FIG. 7.1 Unity. Paul Ranson, Three Beeches, 1905. Oil on canvas, 81.28 × 65.09 cm. Copyright in the Public Domain.

Variety is the use of variation within a composition that provides visual interest. If we go back to the meadow with the cows, the differences in each cow, some with head down, some looking to the side, some with spots and some not, would all be ways of showing variety within a unified composition.

In the composition *Ballet Rehearsal on Stage* by Edgar Degas, Degas has created a very unified composition that provides enough variety to create visual interest. The color palette in this painting is very subdued, yet each portion of the ballerinas clearly stands out against a very neutral background. Each ballerina is unique and therefore provides a sense of variety in what would otherwise be a very drab composition. In true Degas fashion, the center of the composition is empty, and the positioning of the ballerinas forms a clear diagonal line through the composition. However, the interest in this composition is provided by the fact that each of these ballerinas is distinct and interesting in and of herself (Figure 7.2).

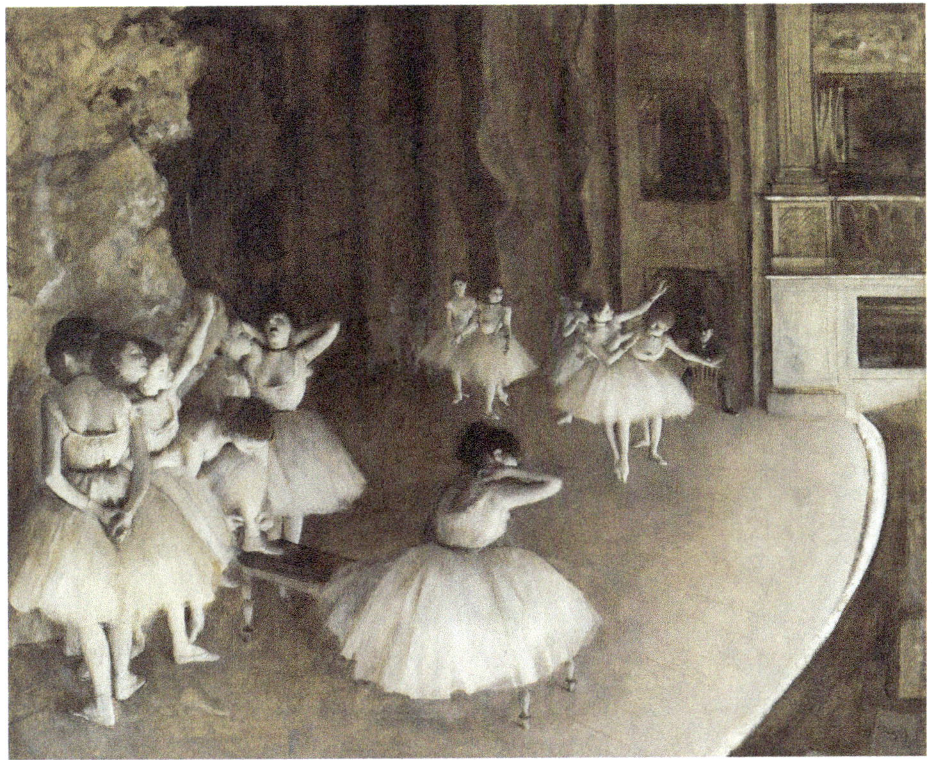

FIG. 7.2 Variety. Edgar Degas, Ballet Rehearsal on Stage, 1874. Oil on canvas, 65 × 81cm. Musée d'Orsay. Copyright in the Public Domain.

PROJECT IDEAS

Creating Unity (and its Opposite)

Unity is the idea that all parts of the composition function together as a harmonious whole and that no one part of the composition stands out as being "odd" or "unusual." Variety adds to the visual interest by creating subtle differences in the objects within the composition. For example, if you were to draw a field full of cows, each cow would be subtly different because no two cows look exactly alike. These differences are an example of variety because even though they are all cows (unity), each one is subtly different in pattern, shape, and size (variety). If in your field of cows there was a skyscraper, you would say that the composition wasn't unified because the skyscraper wouldn't logically exist in a field full of cows.

Divide your paper in half. Use one half of your paper to draw a composition that shows unity and the other half to show the same composition that is not unified.

Creating Variety Using Color

Using magazine pages, cut out a collection of all the same object. For example, you could use a collection of lipsticks from a fashion magazine. Using your collected images, create a collage of your object.

Chapter 8

Emphasis and Subordination

DEFINITION AND TYPES

Artists use ***emphasis*** to draw attention to specific areas within the composition. If this is a specific spot or figure, it is referred to as the ***focal point.*** The focal point is the area within the composition that has the most significance. Emphasis can be created through any means of differentiating one portion of the composition from the rest of the work. Size changes, texture, or variations in color are common ways to draw emphasis to an area in a work of art.

The Milk Maid by Johannes Vermeer combines an unusual ***focal point*** as well as ***emphasis and subordination*** to create the image of a woman pouring milk into a bowl. Light streams into the scene through the window at the left of the image. The muted color palette in the background of the image provides an area of subordination, emphasizing the blue and golden yellow of the milkmaid's clothing as it stands out against the muted hues. The focal point of the image, the stream of milk pouring into the bowl, requires the viewer to pay close attention to the various elements of this quiet scene. Named for the Dutch paintings of the 17th century, ***genre paintings*** are traditionally scenes of everyday life. Vermeer's image of the milk maid is an example of a genre painting (Figure 8.1, page 44).

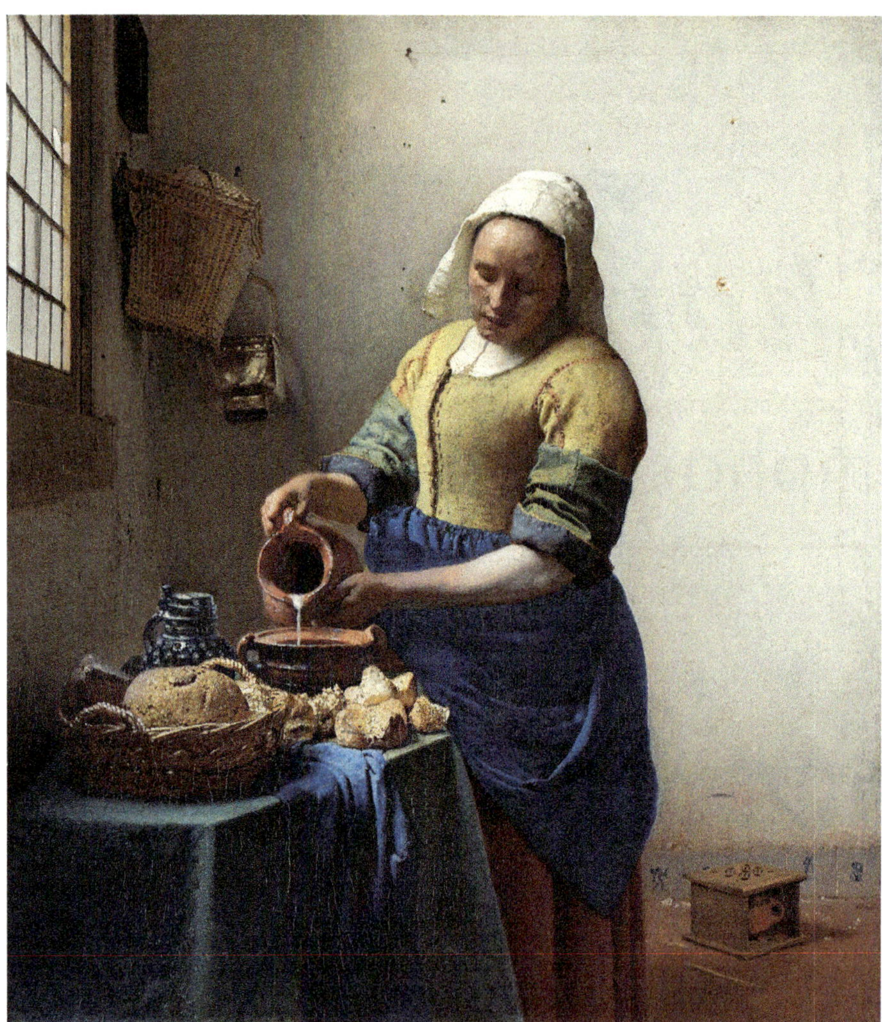

FIG. 8.1 Focal point. Johannes Vermeer, The Milkmaid, 1657-1658. Oil on canvas, 45.5 × 41 cm. Rijksmuseum. Copyright in the Public Domain.

Subordination is the purposeful creation of neutral areas around an area of emphasis to help make the area of emphasis stand out more clearly in the composition. Areas of subordination are meant to help keep the viewer from being distracted from the emphasis of the work.

In *Portrait of Zoe Kambanis,* artist Nikolaos Kounelakis uses the dark background as an area of ***subordination*** against which the luminous skin tone and beautiful gown of the woman shines. The ***focal point***, the wedding ring on her finger, draws the viewer's attention to one of the smaller details of this delicate portrait. The flowers in the vase on the table and the letter on said table provide some visual interest on the left side of the composition and help provide a sense of place and context for the image (Figure 8.2).

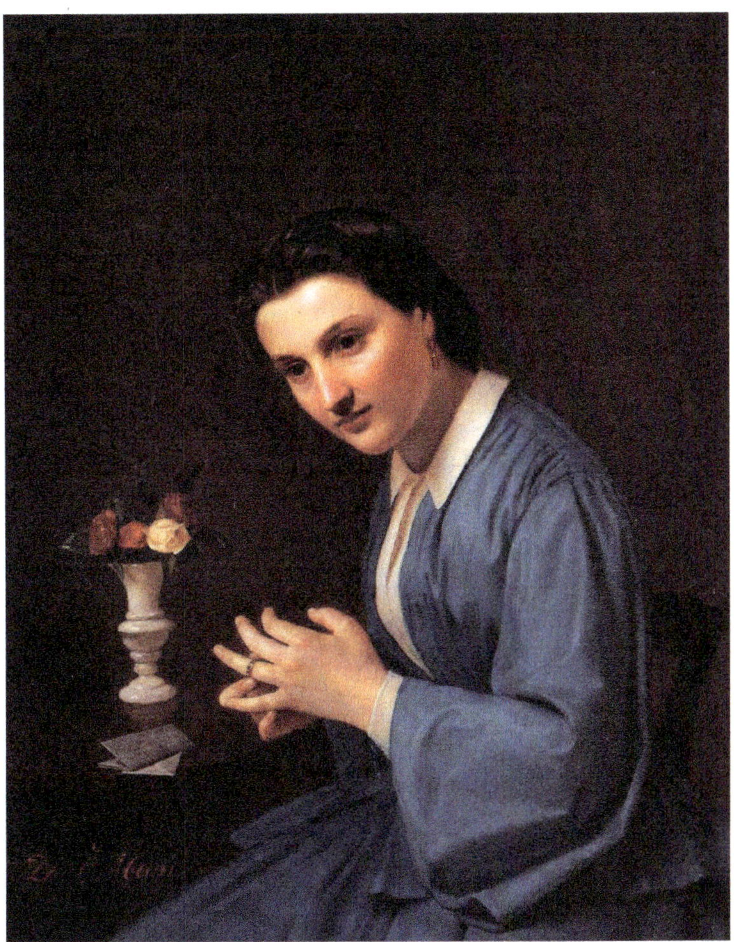

FIG. 8.2 Emphasis and subordination. Nikolaos Kounelakis, Portrait of Zoe Kambanis, 1862. Oil on canvas, 78 × 62cm. National Gallery, Alexandros Soutzos Museum. Copyright in the Public Domain.

PROJECT IDEAS

Focal Point

The focal point of a composition is sometimes called the subject of the composition. The focal point is often identified by its location within the composition or the lack of objects in the surrounding area. If you drew a bowl of fruit against a plain background, then the bowl of fruit would be the focal point, and the area surrounding the bowl of fruit would be the area of subordination.

Using watercolor paint, paint the paper a solid color. Then, using a magazine or a photograph, cut out an image that is of interest to you. Glue the image to the paper. Draw in other objects around the focal point, but be careful not to create too much visual interest beyond your focal point. For example, if you drew a table under your bowl of fruit, it would not make the bowl of fruit less of a focal point, but it would provide more visual interest to the overall composition.

Creating Emphasis Through Color

Draw a composition that has a variety of objects within it. Using complementary colors, color the background in using shades and tints of one color and color the focal point using its opposite color (i.e., color the background in shades and tints of green and the focal point in shades of red). Complementary colors enhance the vibrancy of one another, thereby making the focal point stand out more than it would have otherwise.

Chapter 9
Balance

DEFINITION AND TYPES

Balance is the distribution of visual weight in a composition and can be created using the subject matter of the artwork, color, texture, or space. Balance provides a sense of stability in the composition and can make the design appear stable. There are three types of balance: symmetrical, asymmetrical, and radial.

Symmetrical balance is the matching, or near matching, of each side of the composition along an axis. All of the elements in the composition are similar on each side of the work. In art there is less of a focus on exact symmetry, so if a work is *mostly* symmetrical we refer to it as symmetrical.

In this portrait of *The Qing Dynasty Consort Yehonara* (page 48) we see an example of symmetrical balance. The entire focus of the portrait is on the figure; the background provides an area of subordination, so the entire emphasis is on the Consort. This portrait features almost perfect symmetrical balance with the only differences being subtle variation in the kimono the Consort is wearing. The symmetry is along a vertical axis that runs through the center of the composition with each side almost exactly mirroring the other (Figure 9.1).

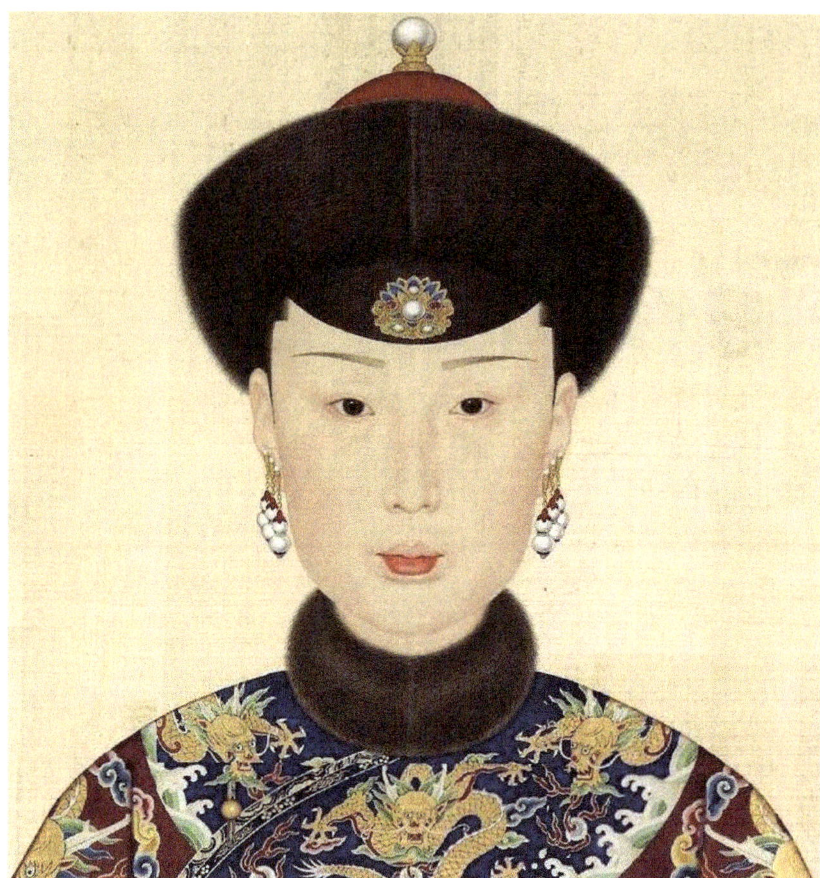

FIG. 9.1 Symmetrical balance. Giuseppe Castiglione and Others, The Official Imperial Portrait of Qing Dynasty's Imperial Consort Yehonara. Handscroll ink and color on silk. Copyright in the Public Domain.

Asymmetrical balance is an uneven distribution of objects, color, texture, or space within the composition. The overall composition still appears balanced, but the two sides are unequal. ***Radial*** balance occurs when the elements are arranged around a central point. A mandala is an example of radial balance, as is a nautilus shell.

This mandala is an example of radial symmetry. This mandala is clearly divided into four equal sections around a center image. The center form inside the circle is then inside another circle inside a square inside a circle inside a square. The repeated motif of circles and squares forms the underlying geometry of this mandala and provides a strong composition upon which to place the Buddhas (Figure 9.2).

Symmetrical balance tends to look more formal while asymmetrical balance looks more relaxed due to the uneven visual weight distribution within the composition.

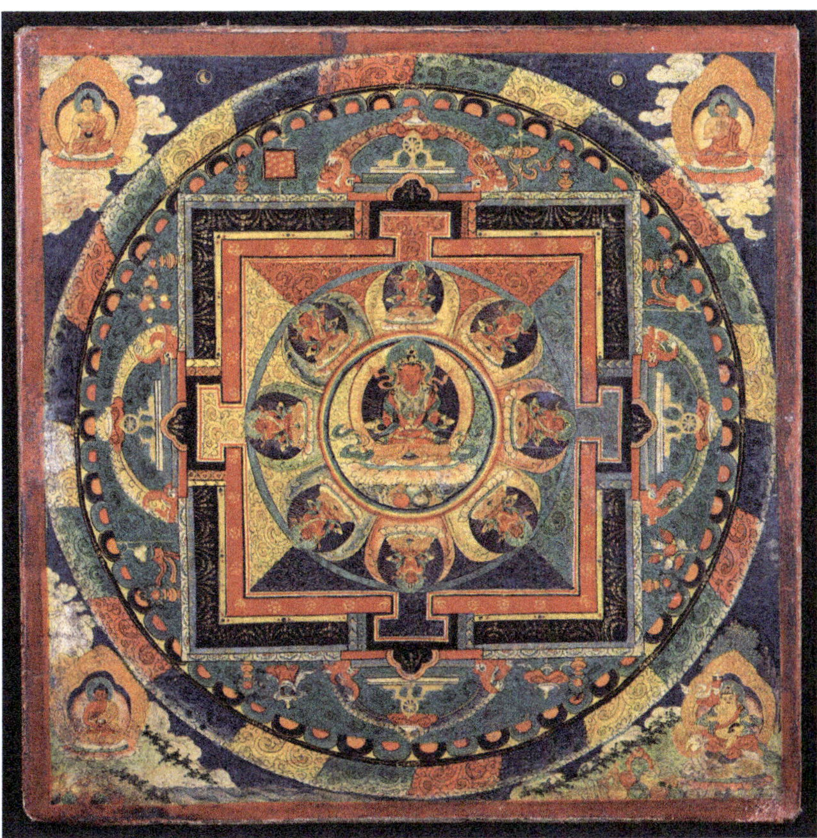

FIG. 9.2 Radial balance. Amitayus Mandala, 19th century. Paint on wood, 31.1 × 31.1 cm. Rubin Museum of Art. Copyright in the Public Domain.

PROJECT IDEAS

Symmetrical Balance (Objective or Non-Objective)

Symmetrical balance occurs when each half of a composition exactly matches the other half. In art, true symmetrical balance is rare, so we tend to think of a composition as symmetrical when each half of the composition *mostly* matches the other half. Slight variation in the exact matching of each half of a composition would not be considered enough to state that a composition is not symmetrical.

Fold a piece of construction paper in half and cut out a shape. The more intricate the shape the more interesting the overall composition will be. Your shape should have a minimum of four interior holes of varying sizes. After the shape is cut out, glue it to a background paper (Figure 9.3).

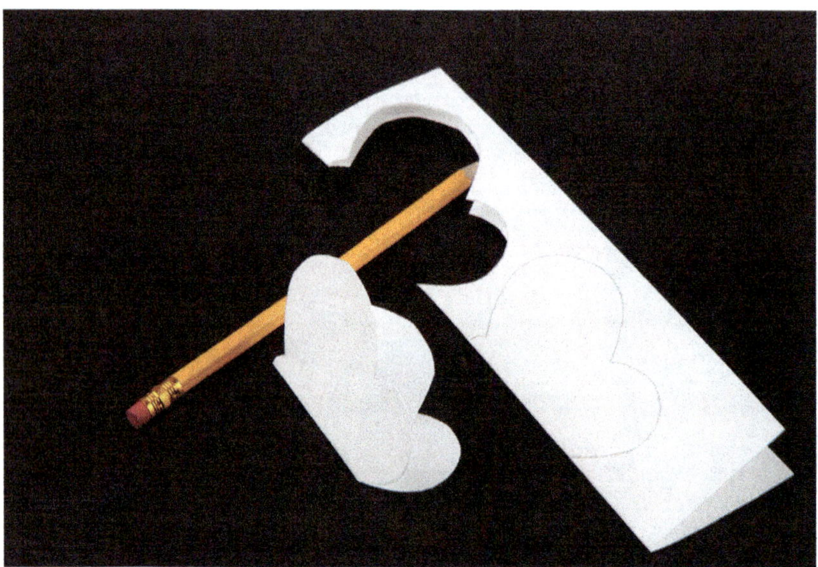

FIG. 9.3 Copyright © Depositphotos/belchonock.

Asymmetrical Balance

Asymmetrical balance occurs when the objects within a composition do not match exactly along the centerline. This can be emphasized by using a strong diagonal line within the composition with the visual weight located in the lower portion of the composition. Asymmetrical balance is considered less formal and more dynamic than symmetrical balance because it creates more visual interest within the composition.

Create a composition where all of the visual weight is located in the lower portion of the paper. Make sure that the subject matter you use is not in the center of the composition as that will make the composition appear more symmetrical even if it is not.

Radial Balance

Radial balance is a type of balance that is based on a circle with its design extending from the center. A starfish, a wheel with spokes, a snowflake, a flower with a center such as a daisy, a stained glass rose window, and a mandala would be considered to have radial balance (Figure 9.4).

To create an image with radial balance first draw a circle as large as the paper will allow in the center of the paper. Divide the circle into four equal pieces. Draw a design in one section. The drawing can be either simple or complex. The drawing must touch the edge of the section at least twice. The design should then be transferred exactly to each of the other three pieces of the circle creating a radial design. Draw over the design with black marker and fill in with colored pencil, being careful to duplicate

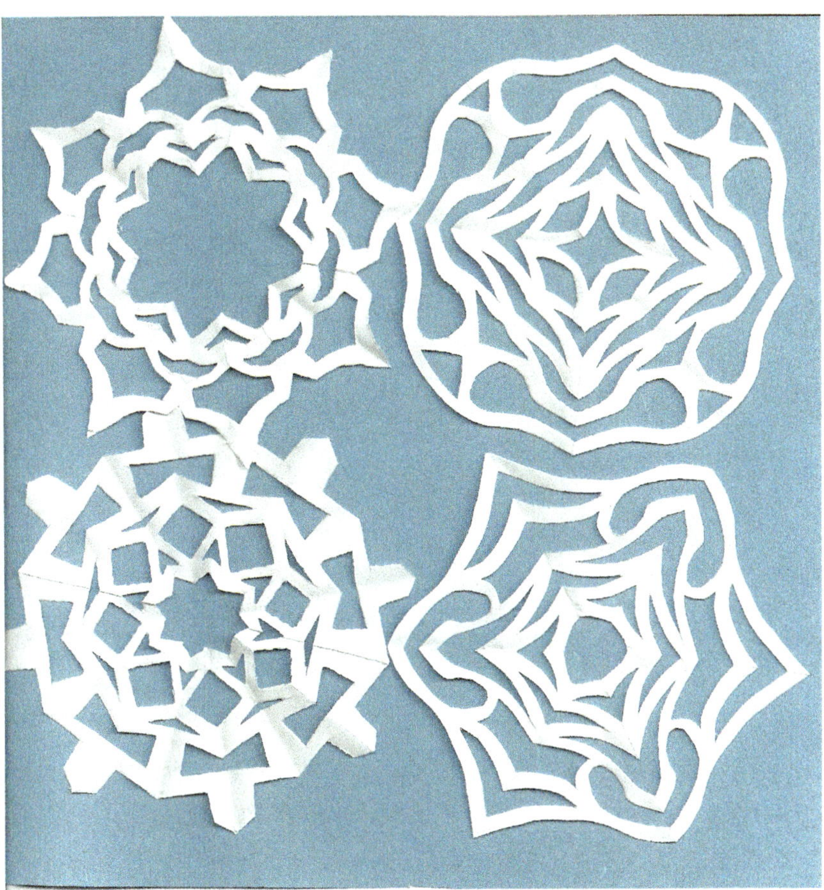

FIG. 9.4 Copyright © IlexSythe (CC BY-SA 3.0) at https://commons.wikimedia.org/wiki/File:PaperSnowflakes Example.jpg.

the color scheme in each section exactly. Dividing the original circle into more than four equal pieces will result in a more involved and interesting final design.

Chapter 10
Rhythm and Repetition

DEFINITION AND TYPES

Repetition is the use of a repeated element within a composition. ***Rhythm*** is a way establishing a visual sense of movement within a composition that combines repeated elements with variation. Rhythm is used as an organizational element within a work of art.

Morning Glories, a six-panel folding screen by Japanese artist Kiitsu Suzuki is a simple image of flowers against a gold background. The visual ***repetition*** of the morning glories provides a sense of ***rhythm*** throughout the image, flowing from each panel of the screen to the next in a delicate curving motion which draws the viewer's eyes from one end of the composition to the other. Rhythm, in this instance, is not the same as pattern since the variation in the design is what makes the overall effect visually interesting. Actual motion, made by standing the screen up in an accordion fashion, enhances the sense of rhythm in the composition. The simple gold background provides an area of subordination against which all the emphasis in the composition is on the morning glories (Figure 10.1).

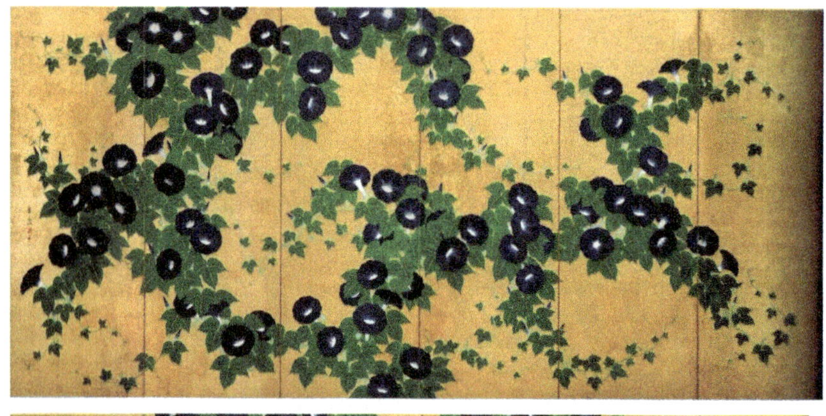

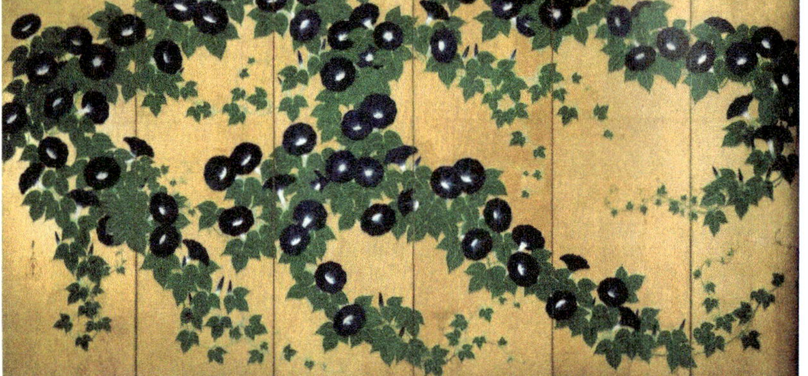

FIG. 10.1 Rhythm and repetition. Kiitsu Suzuki, Morning Glories, early 19th century. Pair of folding screens. Metropolitan Museum of Art. Copyright in the Public Domain.

Pattern is a repeated design motif found in a work of art. It can be as obvious as a checkerboard floor or as subtle as the use of squares to form the underlying compositional structure. Pattern is created through the use of color, line, or shape.

Still Life: Flowers by Pierre Auguste Renoir uses a variety of patterns (a repeated design element) to create visual interest without detracting from the flowers that are the focal point of the image. The table top with its pattern of squares, the tapestry behind the flowers with its patter of diamonds, and the wallpaper with its smaller squares are all painted using a similar color palette and are very muted. The flowers, in contrast to the patterns in the background, are in a more intense, if similar, color palette. The overall effect is a harmonious whole, where no one object stands out as being unusual, and all work together to form an interesting composition (Figure 10.2).

The traditional Bhutanese women's dress *kira kushuthara* uses ***geometric patterns*** to provide interest in the garment. The kira is the national dress of the women of Bhutan. It is a long dress that is wrapped and folded around the body and pinned at both shoulders with brooches. A short jacket and long belt generally complete this traditional ensemble. The kushuthara type of kira is the most highly revered and is traditionally only worn by royalty and on special occasions (Figure 10.3).

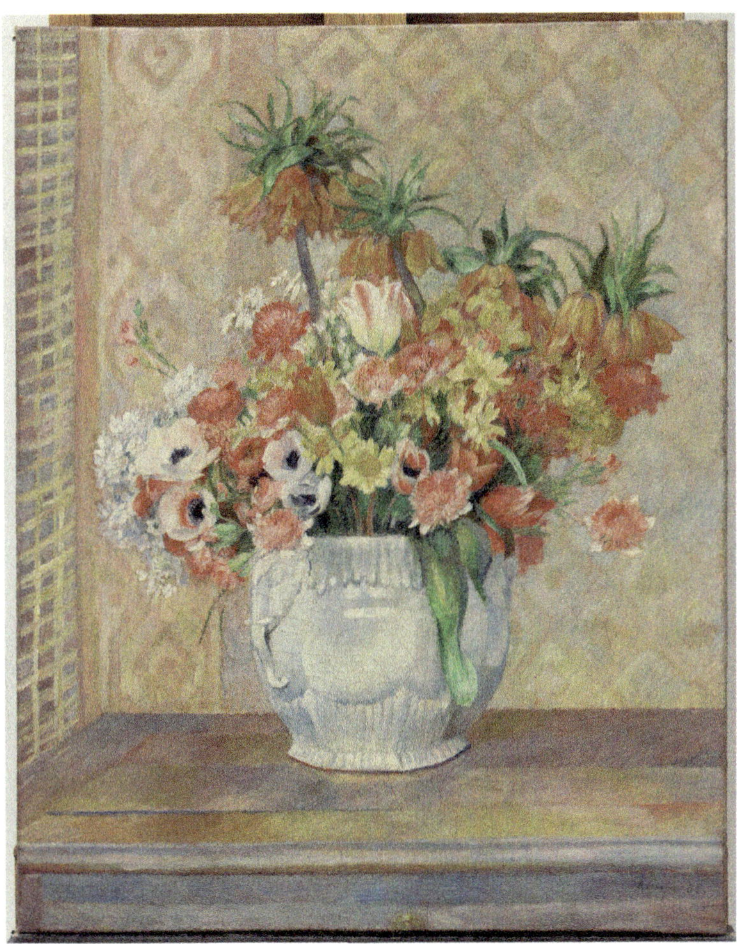

FIG. 10.2 Pattern. Pierre August Renoir, Still Life: Flowers, 1885. Oil on canvas, 81.9 × 65.8 cm. Solomon R. Guggenheim Musuem. Copyright in the Public Domain.

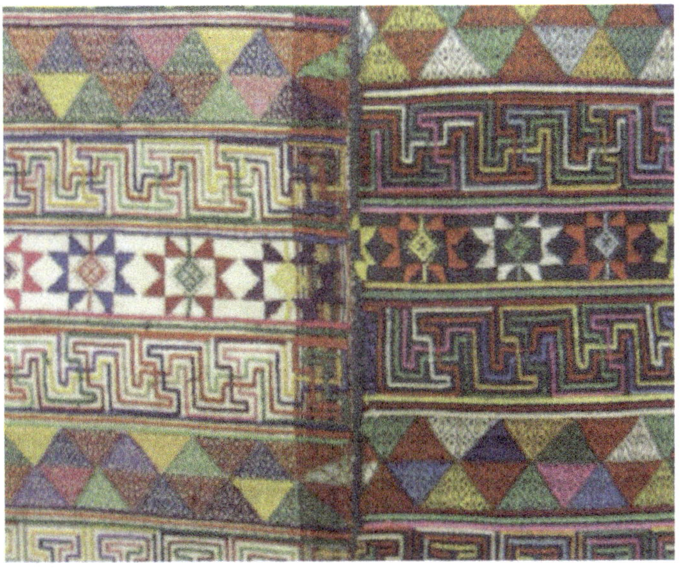

FIG. 10.3 Pattern. Kira kushuthara (woman's dress), early 20th century. Cotton and silk with supplementary weft. Honolulu Academy of Arts. Copyright in the Public Domain.

PROJECT IDEAS

Using Pattern and Color

Create a complex pattern on your paper, using all of the available space. Using color, create a repeating pattern of color. The use of pattern and repetition will create a visual rhythm in the composition.

Using Shape

Repetition of shape is an easy way to establish rhythm in a composition (Figure 10.4). Using a repeating shape is as easy as cutting out a string of paper dolls. Take a piece of construction paper and accordion pleat it, with each pleat a minimum of two inches. This should result in six folds if the paper is pleated horizontally. Draw a simple outline of a person, making sure that one of the hands and one of the feet is touching the crease of the paper. Cut through all six layers at once, creating a string of people holding hands. Attach the string of paper dolls to the background paper. For visual interest you could decorate the background paper with a basic landscape prior to gluing the dolls in place.

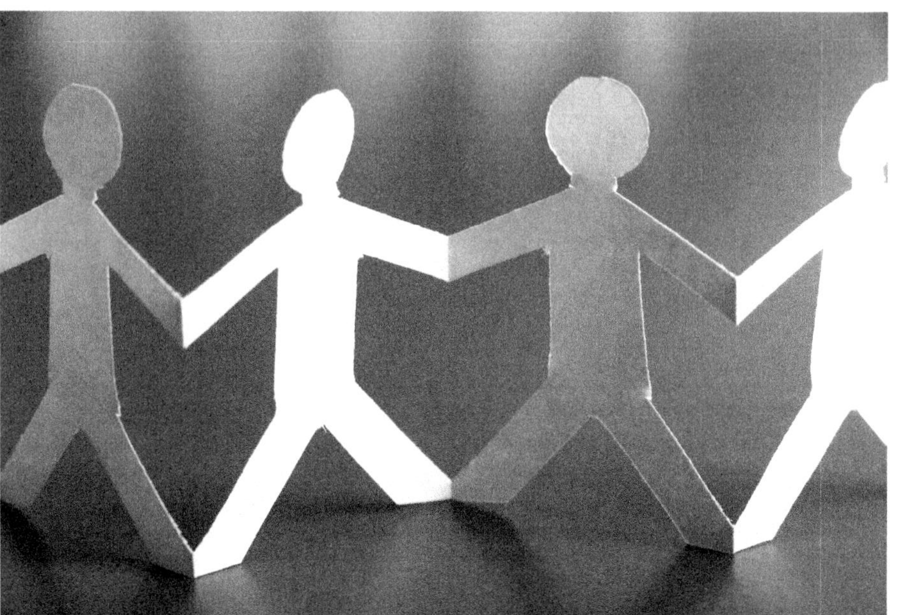

FIG. 10.4 Copyright © Depositphotos/ChristianChan.

Using Ideas

Any idea repeated throughout the composition can function as a means of establishing rhythm and repetition. If you were to draw a line of birds on a power line, the birds themselves would cause a sense of visual rhythm in the composition, drawing your eye from one side to the other. Subtle differences in each bird will provide visual interest. Create an example of rhythm by using a similar idea repeated throughout your composition.

Chapter 11

Contrast

DEFINITION AND TYPES

Contrast is the juxtaposition of strikingly dissimilar elements within a composition. Light versus dark, large versus small shapes or forms, and smooth versus rough textures can all be used effectively to create visual interest, excitement, or drama within a composition. Contrast is often used by artists to draw attention to a particular portion or point of interest within a composition. Contrast within a composition can be created using pattern, color, shape (organic v. geometric), value (dark, light, middle), texture, size (large v. small), and movement.

Contrast is also the juxtaposition of dissimilar elements in the same image. Soft/hard, small/large, black/white, and rough/smooth are just a few examples of the types of contrast that an artist can utilize in a composition. In *Zwiastowanie,* a block print by Jan Panienski, the artist has used a high-contrast color scheme to create a simple abstract image of the Annunciation (Figure 11.1, page 60).

While using black and white would provide the greatest degree of contrast, complimentary colors (opposites on the color wheel) would also provide a very high-contrast surface. Alternatively, analogous colors (adjacent on the color wheel) would provide a low-contrast surface. Warm and cool colors can also be used effectively to provide contrast within a composition.

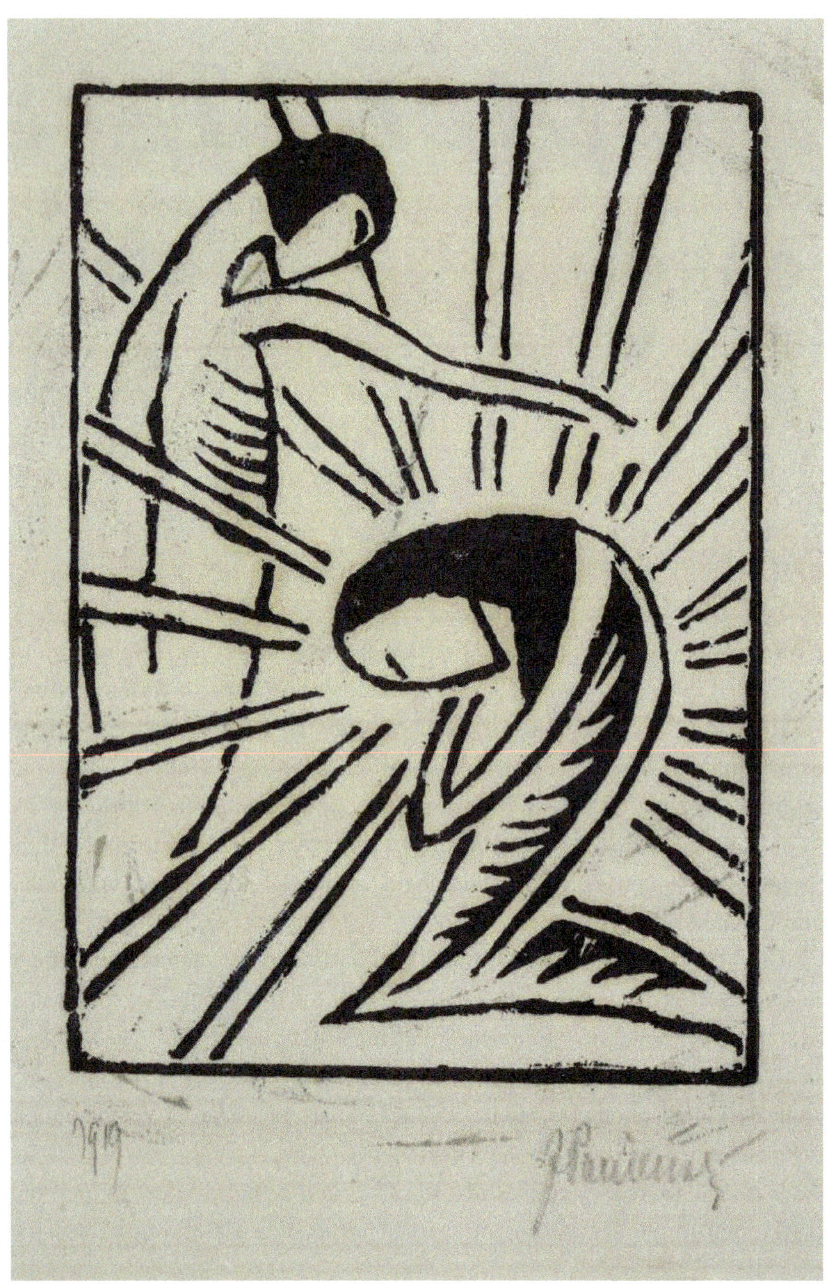

FIG. 11.1 Contrast. Jan Panieński, Zwiastowanit (Annunciation), 1919. Ink print. Copyright in the Public Domain.

PROJECT IDEAS

Figure/Ground Reversal

A figure/ground reversal is created when the viewer cannot establish the difference between the foreground and the background as there is no reference point for establishing the difference between the two. This is easiest to establish by using non-objective shapes, but it is possible to create a figure/ground reversal using identifiable objects. For excellent examples of figure/ground reversal look at the work of M.C. Escher as a reference. Geometric patterns can function in this way due to the inability to differentiate between the foreground and the background in such designs.

Using a piece of colored construction paper, cut out an abstract shape and attach it to the background paper. The shape cut out must not be a recognizable object or it will serve as a focal point rather than a figure/ground reversal.

Using Texture

Texture is an easy way to establish contrast. The difference between smooth paper and sandpaper, for example, provides a contrast that is easy to understand. Using two very different textures, create a design that uses contrast as the primary principle.

Using Color

Color can be used in a high-contrast way (complementary colors) or a low-contrast way (analogous colors). Using one of the aforementioned color schemes, create a simple design that uses either high- or low-contrast color.

Chapter 12

Scale and Proportion

DEFINITION AND TYPES

Scale is the size relationship of one object to another. In the work of Claus Oldenburg, for example, the artist makes excellent use of scale. Objects that we know logically are small in size, such as a clothespin, a shuttlecock, or an apple core, are increased to a gigantic size, making them stand out sharply from their environment due to the sheer absurdity of their existence. Such relationships automatically draw the viewer's attention because they do not exist in the real world. An apple core is not fifteen feet tall nor a shuttlecock eighteen feet tall. The viewer pays attention to the objects because of the scale relationship used by the artist. Scale varies depending on the size of the objects surrounding the primary object, and scale can be easily manipulated.

In the sculpture *Eau de Cologne,* created by the contemporary artist Toyah, scale is the dominant principle of design present (Figure 12.1, page 64). *Scale*, or the size relationship between one object and another, is an area in which artists often play, particularly when making easily recognizable works of art. In this piece, the visual interest is provided by the sheer size of the perfume bottle relative to the size of an actual bottle of perfume. The faithful reproduction of the original object plays up this sense of unreality the viewer experiences when confronted with a bottle of perfume that is significantly larger than the average adult.

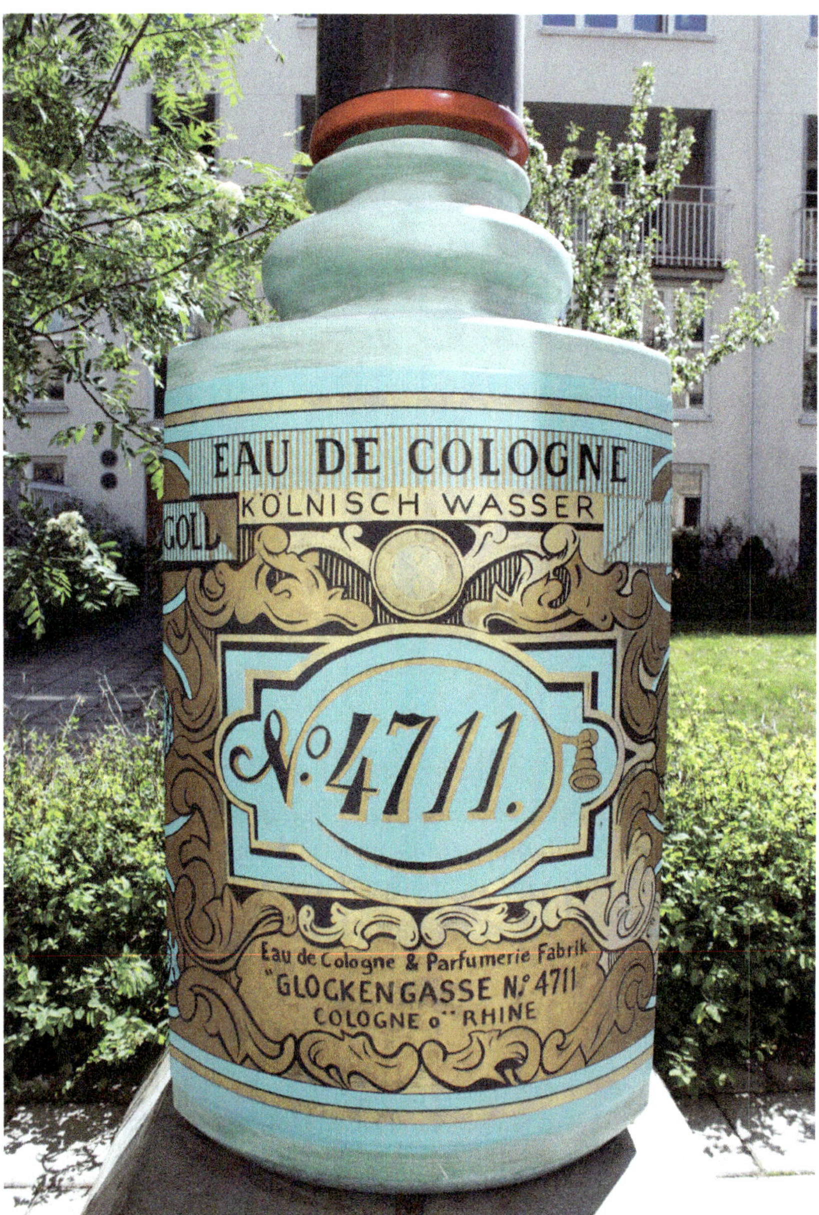

FIG. 12.1 Scale. Toyah, Eau de Cologne, https://commons.wikimedia.org/wiki/File:4711_sculpture.jpg. Copyright in the Public Domain.

When this type of scale relationship is used to define the relative importance of a figure or person, then it is referred to as ***hierarchical scale***. For example, if in a portrait of Jesus and the disciples Jesus is shown as significantly larger than the other figures, then the logical conclusion for the viewer to draw is that Jesus is the most important figure in the image.

In this portrait painting of Kaiser Otto III, Reichenauer Schule has created an excellent example of hierarchic scale (Figure 12.2). If you look closely at the Kaiser, you should note that he is substantially taller than

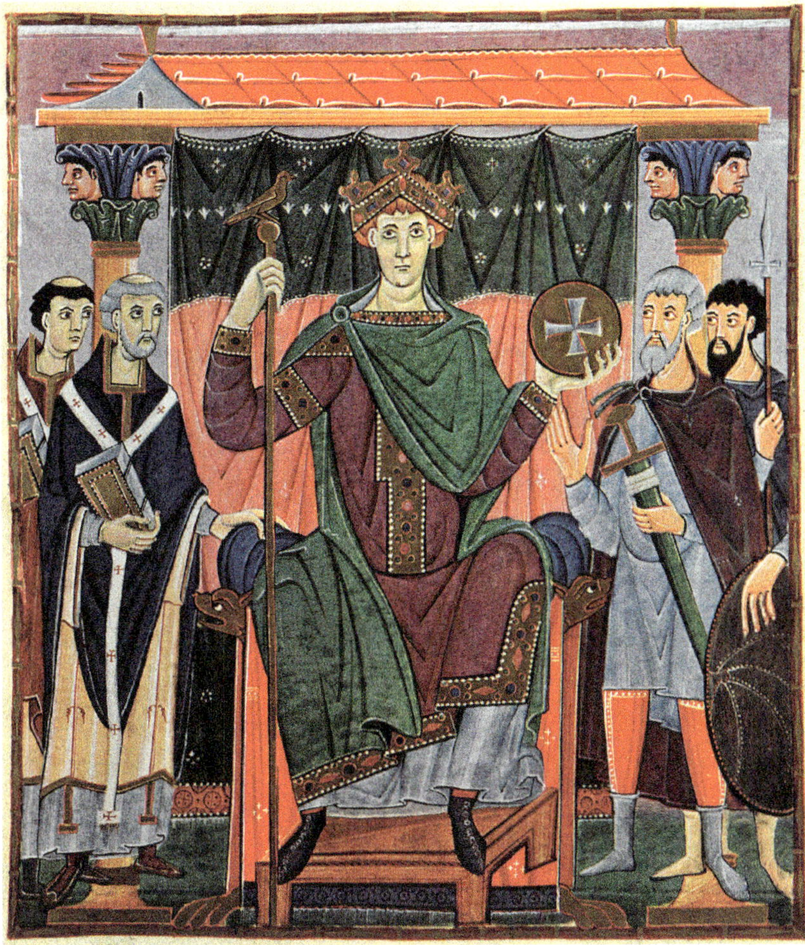

FIG. 12.2 Hierarchic scale. Master of Reichenaurer School, Evangeliar Kaiser Ottos III, ca. 1000. Parchment, 33.5 x 24 cm. Bavarian State Library. Copyright in the Public Domain.

his contemporaries if he were to stand up. This increase in size is meant to indicate his relative importance compared to the other figures in the composition and is a classic example of hierarchical scale in a work of art.

Proportion is the relationship between parts and the whole. If an artist elongates the neck of a person he or she is drawing, then the artist is playing with the proportions of that person relative to reality. ***Foreshortening*** is a type of proportion relationship that artificially shortens the proportions to create the illusion that an object is extending forward in space. For example, if you were painting a person lying on a bed with his or her feet facing toward you, then you would make the feet larger than the other parts of the body to indicate that the feet are closest to you and maximize the illusion of depth within the image.

Self Portrait, Yawning by Joseph Ducreux shows the technique of foreshortening to excellent effect. Foreshortening is a technique that changes the proportions (the size relationship of one part of an object to another part of the object) to make it appear as if it is projecting forward in space on the two-dimensional picture plane. In this case the proportions of the figure's arm are artificially shortened from shoulder to elbow to create the effect of his arm coming forward in space. The reason for this changing of proportion is that to portray actual proportions would actually appear more awkward than artificially changing the proportions so that the image appears "right" to the viewer (Figure 12.3).

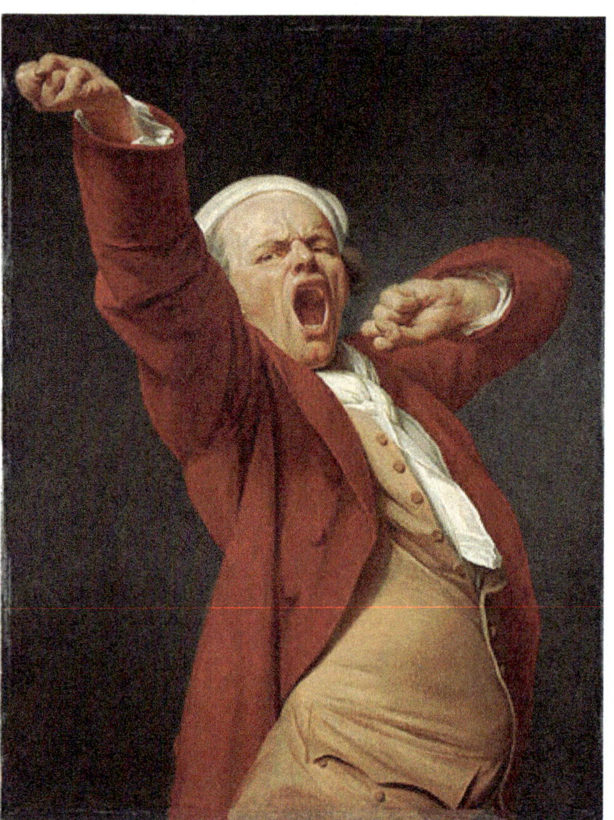

FIG. 12.3 Foreshortening (proportion). Joseph Ducreux, Self-Portrait, 1783. Oil on canvas, 45 x 35 cm. Getty Center. Copyright in the Public Domain.

PROJECT IDEAS

Scale Relationships

Scale is the size relationship between objects. For example, if you were to line up a row of basketballs, and in your row of basketballs you put a golf ball that was the same size as the basketball, you would be playing with the scale since a golf ball is universally acknowledged to be smaller than a basketball. Artists that use scale as their primary focus, such as Claus

Oldenburg, rely on the idea that changing the scale of the object provides visual interest and can create interest in everyday objects.

Using the definition above, create a scale relationship where one object is out of scale relative to the other objects in the composition.

Proportion Relationships

Proportion is the size relationship between parts and the whole. If you were to draw a self-portrait, and one ear was substantially larger than the other, you would be playing with the proportion of the ear relative to the overall size of the head. Varying the proportions of objects within a composition can provide visual interest or create a focal point within the work.

Create a self-portrait that uses unnatural proportions.

Discussion Questions

1. Find an example of hierarchic scale and discuss how the work meets the criteria for hierarchic scale.

2. List five contemporary artists who work in three-dimensional design and what type of work they produce. Provide links to their artist websites.

3. Find an example of an artwork that includes at least two different line weights.

4. Provide five examples of implied texture in artwork from the Renaissance period. Compare these examples to actual texture.

5. Find examples of artwork using each of the following color schemes: monochromatic, analogous, complementary, and triadic. List the artist and medium used in each work.

6. Provide three examples of contrast in real life and compare them with implied contrast in works of art.

7. Find an example of an artwork that does not have unity and discuss why it does not have unity.

8. List five works of art with a strong focal point and describe why each piece meets that criteria.

9. Compare and contrast the differences between linear and atmospheric perspective using two works of art as examples.

10. Discuss the proportions of a work of architecture.

11. List five examples of pattern in real life and five examples of pattern in an artwork.

12. Find 3-5 artists who work in an online medium. Discuss one artist's work in depth. Provide a link to his or her work.

13. Discuss the differences between open and closed form. Cite at least one example from two different cultures.

14. Find an example of time-based artwork such as a comic or graphic novel and discuss how the artist shows the passage of time in the work.

15. Find an example of two-dimensional space and compare it to an example of sculpture that uses space.

References

Appel, Kathy. "The Color Wheel and Color Theory: Important Tools for Interior Design." *Examiner.com*. July 6, 2010. http://www.examiner.com/article/the-color-wheel-and-color-theory-important-tools-for-interior-design.

Blumberg, Naomi. "Linear Perspective." *Encyclopædia Britannica*. March 17, 2016. http://www.britannica.com/art/linear-perspective.

DeWitte, Debra, Larmann, Ralph, and Shields, M.Kathryn. *Gateways to Art.* (New York: Thames & Hudson, 2012).

"Elements of Art." *Getty.edu.* Accessed November 1, 2015. https://www.getty.edu/education/teachers/building_lessons/elements_art.pdf

Fichner-Rathus, Lois. *Understanding Art.* Boston: Wadsworth Publishing, 2012.

Frank, Patrick. *Prebles' Artforms (10th edition).* Boston: Prentice Hall, 2011.

Getlein, Mark. *Living With Art (10th edition).* New York: McGraw Hill Education, 2012.

Handwoven Textile from Bhutan, 1999. Textile. Powerhouse Museum Collection,Sydney, Australia. http://www.powerhousemuseum.com/collection/database/?irn=360567.

Kleiner, Fred. *Gardner's Art Through the Ages.* Boston: Wadsworth Publishing, 2015.

Lamp, Lucy. "Elements of Art: Light." *Sophia*. 2015. https://www.sophia.org/tutorials/elements-of-art-light)

Lewis, Richard and Susan. *The Power of Art.* Boston: Wadsworth Publishing, 2008.

Irving, Bruce. "Light optics for kids: What is light?" *Synopsys*. October 18, 2015. http://optics.synopsys.com/learn/kids/optics-kids-light.html).

Meagher, Jennifer. "Genre Painting in Northern Europe." In *Heilbrunn Timeline of Art History*. New York: The Metropolitan Museum of Art, 2000–. April 2008. http://www.metmuseum.org/toah/hd/gnrn/hd_gnrn.htm.

"Principles of Design." *Getty.edu.* November 1, 2015. https://www.getty.edu/education/teachers/building_lessons/principles_design.pdf.

"Chiaroscuro." *Random House Dictionary*. 2015. *http://dictionary.reference.com/browse/*chiaroscuro.

Richardson, John. *Art: The Way It Is.* Boston: Prentice Hall, 1992.

Strickland, Carol. (1992). *The Annotated Mona Lisa.* Riverside, New Jersey: Andrew McMeel Publishing, 1992.

"The Principles of Design." *j6design.com.* October 15, 2015. http://www.j6design.com.au/6-principles-of-design/.

Tyldesley, Joyce. Isis: Egyptian Goddess. Britannica.com. November 11, 2014. http://www.britannica.com/topic/Isis-Egyptian-goddess.

CPSIA information can be obtained
at www.ICGtesting.com
Printed in the USA
LVOW02s1015060717
540429LV00003BA/15/P

9 781516 505807